Debutante

CultureAmerica

KARAL ANN MARLING / ERIKA DOSS

series editors

Karal Ann Marling

Debutante

RITES AND REGALIA OF AMERICAN DEBDOM

 UNIVERSITY PRESS OF KANSAS

Published by the

University Press of Kansas

(Lawrence, Kansas 66049),

which was organized by the

Kansas Board of Regents and

is operated and funded by

Emporia State University,

Fort Hays State University,

Kansas State University,

Pittsburg State University,

the University of Kansas, and

Wichita State University

Photographs without credit lines come from periodicals
and paper ephemera in the holdings of the libraries of
the University of Minnesota. Three-dimensional objects
are in the collection of the author. Photographs were
prepared for publication by the Visual Resources Center,
College of Liberal Arts, University of Minnesota, through
the good offices of Ashley Wilkes, Ginny Larson, and
Rebecca Moss. Photographic expenses were defrayed by
several generous grants from the Department of Art
History.

Library of Congress Cataloging-in-Publication Data
Marling, Karal Ann.
    Debutante : rites and regalia of American debdom /
Karal Ann Marling.
        p.   cm. — (CultureAmerica)
Includes bibliographical references and index.
        ISBN 0-7006-1317-X (cloth : alk. paper)
        1. Debutantes—United States.   2. Young women—
United States—Social life and customs.   3. United
States—Social life and customs—21st century.   I. Title.
II. Culture America.
HQ1229.M25 2004
305.242′2′0973—dc22   2003023589

British Library Cataloguing-in-Publication Data
is available.

Printed in the United States of America

10 9 8 7 6 5 4 3 2 1

The paper used in this publication meets the minimum
requirements of the American National Standard for
Permanence of Paper for Printed Library Materials
Z39.48-1984.

Contents

How Do I Become a Debutante?

"I want to become a debutante," writes a cyber-society girl. "However, I have found that it is hard to obtain information on the subject. Can anyone tell me . . . more about debuting to society?" Well, if you have to ask, Sweetie, you're probably not "deb" material! Being a deb was and is a rite of exquisite discrimination, of fine distinctions between *our* kind of people and the ones who send plaintive inquiries to web sites. It's about girls—fresh out of finishing or prep school; college freshmen, generally—being introduced to their parents' circle at some formal event of great elegance, expense, or both.

Although the presentees deny it vigorously today, the event is also a coming-of-age ritual, an announcement that the young lady being honored is now of marriageable years and fully equipped with the grace and wisdom to take her place among the cast of eligible college boys, future matrons, maiden aunts, decayed royalty, once-upon-a-time movie stars, tycoons, boring family friends, trophy wives, fortune hunters, and up-and-coming Wall Street bond salesmen invited to the debutante tea/reception/party/ball/cotillion. Or the deb circus (as was the case in 1976, when a Texas daddy with more cash than common sense hired a complete three-ring circus, elephants and all, for his daughter's big night and pitched the tent in the Dallas Convention Center).

For a proper debut, there must be flowers. There's usually a pure white dress of fluffed-up tulle. There may be favors. The circus girl in question gave away five thousand colored balloons with her name on them and five thousand stuffed animals for souvenirs. According to her frazzled mother, the bandleader quit early because he couldn't compete with the elephants, but the party roared on anyway until 1 A.M., when "we ran out of stuffed animals."

Despite consumerist binges, the essence of coming out, or "bowing to society," as the newspapers used to put it, is ancient and universal—

A modern deb, Miss Jillian Godfrey, makes her bow in Atlanta's "Carnival 2002."
Libby Mohr, Atlanta College of Art

in a word, primitive. Novelist J. P. Marquand called the launching ceremonies he observed in Boston before World War II "introducing the virgin to the tribe." Although Margaret Mead was not herself a deb, she surely recognized an echo of Polynesian puberty rites in the special costumes and curtsies and cotillions of the would-be American aristocracy, as Consuelo and Flora and Muffy promenaded across the pages of *Life* magazine, following arcane rules of etiquette best known to mothers, grandmothers, and great-grandmothers all reared to be perfect debs. The whole debutante scene was coded in the genes, like blue eyes and blonde hair. Muffy and her peers were players in a dynastic drama tricked out in symbols of purity and potential fruitfulness—a dress rehearsal for the gala wedding, which ought to take place during the June immediately following the well-planned Christmastime debut.

In this new millennium, nothing could seem more old-fashioned, more demeaning to the modern, independent young woman. But the custom persists, despite setbacks. In the 1960s and 1970s—the era of the so-called Deb Drought—lots of college girls flatly refused to play along; those who did were apt to come to the ball barefoot. No glass slippers for these tie-dye Cinderellas! If they showed up at all, their hair hung in limp clumps, and their escorts wore dirty sneakers and thrift-shop tuxes. The pace of debbing has picked up considerably since, thanks to a virulent wave of neoconservatism. "Buds" (new and potential debs, that is) come out now because it's fun: "a good time," they say, a special party all for *me,* an affirmation of one's family and "roots." "A class thing" about old families. Money is nice for dresses and stuffed animals and vintage champagne, but "you can't buy your way into society." A debutante is still a cut above the vulgar herd.

Think prom night, all you deb wanna-bes: the dress to die for, the wrist corsage, the limo, the thrill of being a grown-up, if only for one evening. Think confirmation and the fluffy white dress. The Sweet Sixteen party. The bat mitzvah bash, with a Hawaiian theme—or a circus motif. The quinceañera, for the fifteen-year-old Latina. The beauty pageant, in which hopefuls parade across the stage on the arms of handsome young naval officers and bow daintily to the judges. These are puberty-linked, female ceremonials certifying that a girl has become a woman ready for marriage, perhaps, or for an adult role in whatever quadrant of the social spectrum she may find herself. Muffy is ready to get married, go to grown-up parties, drink champagne, advertise face cream and cigarettes, fend off Euro-trash suitors, sing in nightclubs, host charity luncheons, and become a high-powered corporate attorney.

At times in the past two hundred years, the debut has pointed toward one or several of these options. At the end of the nineteenth century, in the heyday of the deb, marriage was the customary dividend from the familial investment in roses and tulle, although the little bud was also expected to display fine manners and occasionally indulge in good works. In the 1930s, debutantes were public figures, fodder for glamorous magazine layouts. "Debs of the Year" were designated by New York gossip columnists. Debs stayed up late, smoked incessantly, and occasionally appeared in Broadway musicals. Jackie Kennedy (née Bouvier) and her sister Lee emerged from the last crop of headline debutantes, who were succeeded by big-money debs, the Deb Drought, the semi-secret deb (who refused to tell her own roommate what she had done over Christmas break), and, in our time, the almost-anybody-can-be-a-deb deb. This last category is composed of ethnic semi-debs, look-alike rituals for middle-class debs, gay male debs, and a long list of similar social hybrids.

So the short, sweet answer to the question of how to become a debutante is this: buy the dress, give a tea party, invite everybody you know, and stand in the entry hall with your mom, shaking hands with the guests. That's all there is to it, according to the oldest etiquette manuals. Bingo! You're out! An even easier method: whenever the family sends out greeting cards, sign your own name in full underneath theirs. This bit of chicanery is known as "slipping out." Alternatively, join a club for Polish-Americans, African-Americans, Ukrainian-Americans, a club of any sort that sponsors an annual debutante showcase, and be very nice to everybody. Have your father make a big donation to the cause. But the long answer is that no closetful of designer gowns, no service club, no tea is going to make you a *real* debutante unless somebody notices, and those bodies have got to be real, bona fide somebodies. Besides, if you have to ask how to do it, Darling, you're probably not good deb material!

But if you're already out there, surfing the web for pointers, the word *debutante* will take you in fascinating directions. To on-line stores specializing in deb regalia, for example. Dresses. Tiaras. Strings of pearls.

White kid above-the-elbow gloves, first worn, according to the chatty manufacturer, in 1870, when a Mr. King of New York City rented Delmonico's ballroom for his daughter's debut—the first ever held in a public venue. The same firm boasts of having custom made gloves for the Misses Bouvier and for actress Michelle Pfeiffer in the 1993 film *The Age of Innocence*. Based on the novel by socialite Edith Wharton, *The Age of Innocence* stars Pfeiffer as the notorious Ellen Olenska. "What can you expect of a girl who was allowed to wear black satin at her coming-out ball?" asks one of her critics. What indeed?

Although a ball is not a hard-and-fast prerequisite for a debut, the waltz-'til-three costuming identifies the deb in the popular imagination. On shopping sites, such as debsontheweb.com, debs constitute a category interchangeable with brides, promgoers, pageant queens, and quinceañeras. And movie stars. But one unique item identifies the North Carolina debutante aiming for presentation by the prestigious Terpsichorean Club of Raleigh. Once upon a time, the marshals (organizers) and the girls gathered outside the Municipal Auditorium before the annual ball began. To protect their gowns, bedsheets were spread on the ground beneath each young lady, and stools were brought out so they could perch without damage to their petticoats while the introductions were being made. Each 2003 Terpsichorean deb had a hand-painted, personalized "deb stool," four-legged, thirty inches high, and adorned in a special design of her own choosing. You can get one, too, for $100, unless the motif is especially complicated (such as a precise copy of an engraved deb party invitation). Then, the price goes up accordingly.

Under the same heading, however, there are scores of pornographic videos for sale or rent, grouped together under the perverse belief that if a naughty deb goes bad, it must be twice as titillating as when plain old Debby does Dallas. There are romance novels set in the Old South, where debutantes and belles flutter their fans in every magnolia-drenched corner of every ballroom. There are books of sophisticated paper dolls from the 1940s: "The Debutantes, Sandra and Sally." Articles about the West Coast punk-rock band called WTD—White Trash Debutantes. Long-winded discussions of how *debuter*, a French word meaning "to lead off," became the American *debutante*. Because, as the guest of honor, she led the cotillion, or danced the first dance of the evening with her proud father? But how did teas and signatures on cards turn into gala balls in the first place? And what's a cotillion, anyway, if it's not just a dressed-up name for a junior prom on its best behavior?

In the chapters that follow, I intend to demystify debdom. Sheer curiosity has a lot to do with my investigations. When I was a little girl, newspapers still had "society pages," with brides, debs, and breathless reports on how rich ladies entertained one another. The decorations were described in minute detail. Guest lists were printed. Menus and bridge scores reported. Dresses gushed over. Oh, the wonder of "a rose silk frock embroidered in silver threads, with a décolleté bodice and flowing tulle sleeves, . . . set off with a bouquet of Thayer roses"! What was a Thayer rose? A décolleté (occasionally spelled *decollette*) bodice? The imagination ran riot. Why were the regal, unsmiling young ladies pictured in their white formals making bows in the first place? Why weren't my mother's Wednesday afternoon card parties ever discussed? We made little sandwiches without crusts and frosted little cakes with pastel icing. Weren't they just as nice as the ones Mrs. Mother-of-the-Deb served? Debuting (debbing?) was one of the great, cosmic imponderables of my childhood, along with why I had to wear ugly brown oxfords when all the other girls had patent leather maryjanes.

This long-term American hankering after the trappings of royalty is another peculiarity of the deb story. Girls chew gum and wear grungy cutoffs in the morning and become Ruritanian princesses by 10 P.M., bedecked in gowns and little crowns, making curtsies that would not have been out of place in the court of Queen Victoria. (And why do deb balls open at the very hour when the rest of us start to yawn and think about bedtime?) Clearly, debbing is a ritual grounded in aspiration, retrospection, and legitimization. America's would-be aristocrats want to reaffirm their blood ties to greatness. They look back to a Cabots-and-Lowells past and decry the pushy energies of plastic surgeons and former Enron executives who would have their own offspring marked with the seal of gentility.

The best part of the whole debutante scene may be that some girls *don't* get picked for the big, splashy affairs that a few newspapers still report on. The ins have the fiendish pleasure of looking down with amused disdain upon the outs, upon the earnest strivers seeking admission to the *Social Register* on the basis of cash contributions, ambitious wives, and pretty daughters. To engineer a successful debut is to place one's faith in the unspoken proposition that the girl in the white dress reifies her parents' standing in the community, launches her career among people who can do her some good along the way, and fortifies Daddy's pleasant feelings of belonging, accomplishment, and having done the right thing.

But if all else fails—if Muffy isn't on the invitation list for the High-and-Mighty Cotillion, despite heroic efforts—then the last resort of the defeated newcomer is to repair to the nearest bar and order up several "Debutante's Dreams." A shot of bourbon, a shot of brandy, another of orange juice. A dash of lemon juice. Pour over ice. Shake: don't stir. Strain into a cocktail glass. Drink several, very quickly. Keep 'em coming, and the nightmare of rejection will soon fade into blessed oblivion.

The Debutante's Dream is a potent elixir—a dream of being almost royalty, a paragon of good taste and elegance, a name to be reckoned with. A collective family dream in which the pretty daughter is both proof of good breeding and a bid to improve the stock through grafting, via a dynastic union between the bud and a worthy sprig from a slightly higher branch on the social tree. The grand society debut of the nineteenth century nonetheless casts the young woman in an essentially ambiguous role. Only yesterday an insignificant schoolgirl, she is suddenly the cynosure of all eyes, the little queen for a day whose every wish amounts to a regal command. And yet she is also a sort of stalking-horse for her family, a pawn, the means whereby their social fortunes may rise or fall. If she is not the belle of the ball, she is, at the very least, expected to attract a decent suitor and spare her father the duty of supporting an "elderly girl," as the post-deb spinster was scornfully called. Ostensibly for and about a daughter, the debut was not really about her at all, except that she became the prime instrument of her own transmutation into obedient wifery.

At the same time, the elaboration of social rites like the debut empowered women at the very historical moment when their tangible contributions to the household were on the wane. In the urban family, father went to the office and mother became the "Light of the Home," its artistic, moral, and social arbiter. In the absence of meaningful, income-producing chores (immigrant labor took care of those), women paid calls on one another, organized gala occasions on which busy industrialists could meet face-to-face, and compensated themselves for

Debs with plumes: a 1903 magazine cover by famous illustrator Harrison Fisher, whose specialty was the American Girl in full flower.

their cosseted roles as domestic goddesses by wielding enormous power in the social realm. They were the autocrats of organized American leisure time, the list-makers, the gatekeepers, the style-setters, the black-ballers. And the debut was one of the most potent weapons in their arsenal of ballroom sovereignty. So the fabled debuts of the Gilded Age demonstrate the nature and the limits of the feminine power, which would gravitate to the ballot box in 1920 with the passage of the Nineteenth Amendment.

But the rash of guidebooks leading the attentive reader through the maze of cabalistic social customs gave hope to the many that they might—with proper instruction—join the fortunate few hosting deb parties at Sherry's and Delmonico's. The fin de siècle years, when the rules of protocol were at their starchiest, also produced a rash of 25¢ manuals showing the would-be deb exactly how to fold down the corner of her calling card, where to stand in a receiving line, what to wear, and how to keep up her end of a conversation. The implication was that anybody could become a member of the elite "400"—the number of socialites who could fit in Mrs. Astor's ballroom in 1892—by following a few simple rules and choosing the right clothes. And superficially, at least, the strategy seemed to have some hope of success.

In a front-page article in the fall of 1893, just as the social "season" was getting started, the *New York Sun* noted the arrest of a young woman at the opera on suspicion of being a notorious "sneak thief," wanted on several continents. What was alarming about the story, and what landed the prisoner on the front page, was her splendid appearance: diamond earrings, a dress of brown figured silk trimmed in three rows of white lace, "dainty French slippers, with a red flower on the toe of each," and a velvet opera cloak edged in fur. Because of her "swell appearance," neither the police nor the audience felt quite right about the public apprehension of a girl who looked every inch the lady. In a culture that placed undue emphasis on appearances—diamonds, an elegant bearing, a good seat at the opera—the revelation of a debutante, resplendent in tulle and pearls, was one more spectacle of adherence to the norms described in the etiquette books.

Stories in the newspapers helped change the perception of what debbing was all about. In the late 1920s and the 1930s, debs acquired press

In one of monologist Ruth Draper's most famous dramatic turns, she played a New York debutante at a dance (1903).

agents. The goal was celebrity, becoming a front-page story, like the criminal/lady of 1893. A wave of deb heiresses, poor little rich girls on the loose in Manhattan's tonier nightclubs, washed over a period when most people were barely getting by. The rich became fairy-tale figures whose antics and amusements distracted readers in Kalamazoo and Cedar Rapids from their own troubles. Like the movie stars with whom they so often mingled, super-debs Barbara Hutton and Brenda Duff Frazier led what seemed to be exciting lives of unrelieved pleasure and material comfort. They were debs to dream of, with their long, blood-red fingernails and their ruby lips. Grace Kelly would play the last of the nightclub babies in 1956's *High Society*, a movie musical based on Philip Barry's prewar Broadway play *The Philadelphia Story* (and an earlier film of the same name). This was Miss Kelly's last cinematic fling: with her cool, debbish demeanor and preppy looks, she became a real princess when she married Prince Rainier of Monaco later that same year. America's Hollywood royalty thus became the genuine article. Or monarchy had at last descended to the status of mere celebrity.

Weddings are part of the bigger debutante picture, too, along with balls, pageants, and splendid parties of all sorts at which the serious business of society (or societies) is transacted. What do they mean? How are they staged? Who calls the shots? What do the participants stand to gain from all the fuss and feathers? How have they changed? Who goes and who can't? And what do they have to do with the proud American girls who schemed and plotted to bow ever so deeply before the reigning monarch of England not so long ago?

It would be wonderful if the history of debdom were crisply linear. If the story moved from Queen Victoria's trend-setting all-white wedding and the sublimely stuffy court presentations of nineteenth-century London to sorority initiations in twenty-first-century America by neat, dainty steps. If young Lady So-and-So bowing to her monarch at Buckingham Palace turned out to be the model for the nervous Kansas coed in a white dress, clutching her candle, as her future "sisters" (already candled and pledged) stand by in black gowns listening to a recitation of her impressive accomplishments. Well, that's true. The sorority girl and the homecoming queen and the promgoer are the distant offspring of young Lady So-and-So—and Victoria's love of ritual and propriety.

But alas, the family tree of the debutante has many gnarly branches. The path across the ballroom floor is far from straight; there are slips, slides, and not-so-graceful arabesques of movement along the way.

In the beginning, there *was* the European aristocracy, nudging their offspring into suitable marital alliances by a series of rites of passage that publicly defined everybody's social standing with some precision. Since the girls were the future mothers of future dukes and earls, and since the mores of the time dictated that they be guarded like the family jewels they were, girls went to court to "come out": to establish their bona fides and to begin a round of socializing during a "season" in London. With any luck at all, they would be satisfactorily married off before the year was out. So first, this chronicle of debbing will take up the court debut—and the Americans who sought both legitimacy and prestige by meeting a foreign queen.

Class has always been a problem in supposedly classless America. In the wake of the Civil War, with the rise of new fortunes, class became an especially pressing issue. Did money and power define the "best" people—or was it a venerable name, going back to the *Mayflower* and the Dutch burghers of New Amsterdam? The great social wars of the fin de siècle period, waged with especial vigor and venom in New York City, ended in an uncomfortable truce. It was possible to assert one's superiority to the common herd by spending the money needed to buy a daughter's debut at the Court of St. James. But, at the same time, less-than-millionaires from good (a.k.a., old) families could introduce their girls to prospective mates of similar breeding by simply holding a tea party at home. Mother wore her best dress. Daughter wore white. Everybody expressed pleasure at meeting everybody else. Friends poured sacramental cups of pale tea. And thereafter, young Edith or Emily or Eleanor was an official woman, free to join in adult company and to assume the burdens thereof: marriage, gentility, and scrupulous observance of the rules of her social set.

Debutante teas did not have to be tedious. If one were bent on attracting notice in a circle wider than that of the matrons who nibbled on scones, the ceremony could be moved to some hoity-toity club and given an infusion of razzle-dazzle. Mother and daughter could order their costumes from the day's hot dressmakers, in the flashiest styles. They could invite lots of men. And a society reporter or two, to describe the charming effect in the newspapers. In other words, the tea readily ceased to be about a family and its friends—a narrow definition of community—and passed into the realm of publicity or celebrity. It is widely accepted among students of the phenomenon that, between 1910 or so and 1950, America experienced a frenzy for fame. Flagpole sitters, movie vamps, golfers, and criminals—the whole motley tribe of them—became household names, thanks to press agentry and picture magazines. Not everyone could be a Babe Ruth or a Theda Bera, but becoming famous for being famous—for having your name and your picture in the paper—was possible for almost anybody prepared to spend a little time and money to steal into the spotlight of public attention. Debutantes were among the first private citizens with no legitimate claim to admiration to occupy that stage on a regular basis. In that sense, Monica Lewinsky and the American debutante may be sisters under the skin!

How to be a deb: One could bow to the queen. Or endure a round of tea parties. Dancing was a third route to making a successful debut. Southern girls did not, on the whole, come out over teapots. Instead, they danced, from Philadelphia on down through Baltimore and Richmond and Atlanta, into New Orleans and the Delta. The "barbecue" at the Twelve Oaks plantation that begins Margaret Mitchell's *Gone with the Wind* could be the venue for any number of Dixie debuts, as girls of marriageable age compete in costume and coquettish "fiddle-dee-dees" for the attention of young beaux, while older and wiser heads ponder the prospects of civil war. The true "belle" cut a fine figure on the dance floor by virtue of her grace, beauty, charming manners, and knowledge of the intricate steps through which she cavorted in figure dances managed by men. In the South—and in places influenced by the Southern style—gallant gentlemen often took the lead in choosing belles for their cotillions, or formal dances.

Elsewhere, however, and particularly in the Northeast, the mothers who had once planned their daughters' teas went on to stage-manage expensive private balls, which became the norm in the 1920s and 1930s, when the antics of dollar celebrities helped distract the nation from its economic and social woes. The fact that debutante millionairesses who dined in swank clubs could sing off-key or hate the whole ballroom scene gave assurance to non-debs reading about their exploits that Brenda and Cobina were pretty much like themselves. The difference between a deb and the daughter of a dairy farmer amounted to accessories and makeup, the very products that debutantes routinely advertised. So, if you bought Pond's cold cream, you could be just like Brenda Frazier—a perfectly ordinary celebrity. A Horatio Alger story for girls, the life cycle of the deb proved that in America, any ambitious young lady with a little luck, pluck, and cold cream could be a star, for a little while. Urban legend has it that Lana Turner was "discovered" by a Hollywood agent while sipping a soda at the lunch counter of a California drugstore: the myth arises from this unshakable American faith in possibility.

The men who picked the dancing debs were not, for the most part, idle fops. They were movers, shakers, and graspers. They lived in the glare of publicity, envied by their employees, often resented by the less fortunate in their communities, and easy targets for mudslingers and anarchists alike. Just as the lodges and orders of the nineteenth century gave men an imaginative retreat from the reality of their days, so did a variety of secret civic societies, which captivated the general public with their mumbo-jumbo and an anonymity protected by bizarre costuming. In New Orleans, masked "krewes" ruled the city during elaborate pre-Lenten festivities. In the Midwest, it was the Veiled Prophets of St. Louis who asserted their hegemony over mere mortals by commandeering city streets for an annual gala, which included a mass debut of their daughters and their friends' daughters. Under the aegis of the mysterious Prophet, debs became queens (American Victorias!) or princesses and, in keeping with the demands of celebrity, were paraded through the city as its official virgins.

It seems important to pay some attention to the debutante rituals of places like St. Louis and Kansas City because, despite the perpetuation of bloodlines and the gratuitous expenditures that make a deb a deb, the stakes may have been just a little lower in the great beyond to the west of the Hudson River—and the events themselves a little more fun. Certainly, there is a more direct correlation between coming out and the good of the community as a whole. The Kansas or Missouri girl in the white dress confers prestige not only on her parents and herself but also on the polity she represents. And that is best accomplished by riding on floats, wearing weird crowns and jewels, and carrying excessively large bundles of flowers (easily seen from a distance).

Sometimes, especially in the Midwest, a queen must compete for attention with a cow or a horse. Or debbing becomes a demonstration of eugenic theory in practice. At the end of the nineteenth century, through the good offices of land-grant universities, the selective breeding of plants and animals became a major rural preoccupation. Fairs gave prizes for cattle bred to rigid standards of girth and shape, and regional business leaders purchased "prize" animals to publicize and encourage the improvement of local agriculture. Applied to human reproduction, these principles led state fairs to hand out trophies for the chubbiest baby—and the prettiest girl—with the clear implication that purity of bloodlines accounted for superiority in people, too. So the eugenics movement, widely discredited after the Nazi horrors of the 1930s and 1940s, takes on a sort of routine, commonsensical flavor in states where agriculture is a primary fact of life. The debutante has a special symbolic importance because, like a blue-ribbon dairy cow bred from blooded stock, her lineage can be traced back to the sturdy, God-fearing founders of today's inland empire.

Charity balls, or debbing in the aid of good works, flourished in the 1940s and 1950s, when even the richest *nouveaux* came to realize that conspicuous consumption without a benevolent purpose invited ridicule and opprobrium. Though the odd deviation from the new norm—Texas debs are a law unto themselves—was inevitably mentioned in the *New York Times,* it was never in complimentary terms. Debbing for a cause, for some purpose beyond self-aggrandizement, had particularly important consequences as the big WASP debut scene began to fade back into the private enclaves from which it had arisen. Black America reacted against the segregated ball by founding unique African-American debutante mechanisms, with a strong emphasis on sustaining traditions of solidarity, scholarship, and responsibility. While a succession of blonde New York society debs frittered away their time in various jet-set escapades, black girls (and their escorts) learned hard lessons about their obligations to other people of color. The debut ceremony attested to their readiness to lead, as professionals and persons of influence in their communities.

Ethnic coming-out parties flourished, too—the hyphenated debut. Girls primped and curtsied and formed giant stars and circles on the dance floor, but they also learned to value the heritage of the countries from which they and their parents had come, if only in the folk melodies of the evening's musical selections. Recently, immigrants from Latin America, Cuba, and Puerto Rico have made the quinceañera, a celebration of the sexual maturity of the fifteen-year-old girl, into a complex deb ritual, adopting many of the traditions of the Vanderbilt-era debut via a different route: namely, the influence of the courts of Spain and France on their own colonial ancestors.

So, at any given time, teas and balls and figure dancing and cram classes in Ukrainian history and mariachi music and civic parades may be happening at once. All of them debuts. All perfectly correct, beautiful, and wonderful. A heady mixture of class, celebrity, and community interests. Sexuality and sociability. The empowerment of women and their subjugation. Debuts are all-American occasions, and yet profoundly foreign. The great American architect and theorist Robert Venturi once wrote a book on buildings he admired because they were, he said, both complex and contradictory. So is coming out. Muffy, the aspiring debutante, is cautioned, then, that the chronology of this story is sometimes serpentine, if not circular; that decorous teas are being held even as trust-fund debs are getting tipsy on bathtub gin; that today's prom queens are every bit the equal of the No. 1 Deb of 1938; and that, Dear Muffy, *of course* you can become a deb!

CHAPTER ONE *Fuss & Feathers*
Making a Bow to Royalty

ith his report on the doings of the Babylonian aristocracy, the ancient historian Herodotus became the first to describe what is now known as a debut. Those with marriageable daughters brought them once a year, he said, "to a place where a great number of men gathered about them." There they were auctioned off to the highest bidders, beginning with the prettiest. But the bill of sale was drawn up "only on condition that the buyers married them." This could be a thumbnail sketch of the typical English presentation ceremony of the nineteenth century.

Kings and queens, to be sure, had traditionally demanded that courtiers and peers (and their nubile daughters) attend upon them: royal levees were just that—receptions at which the monarchy could view its subjects, and vice versa. During the reign of George II, almost anyone with a decent suit of clothes could appear at court of an evening to watch the royals play cards. But rules were pickier for introductions or "presentations." The Georges, on the advice of the College of Heralds, permitted no illegitimate daughters to be introduced, unless respectably married. His Majesty kissed all the ladies who bowed daintily before him; the Queen, only daughters of earls and the higher nobility.

Before the American Revolution, fashionable colonials sometimes took their female offspring to London for presentation, in hopes of snaring a rich and titled son-in-law at court. For a time after the rebels expelled Cornwallis from the now–United States, however, patriots disdained such gestures of obeisance to the former enemy, even when the niceties of diplomacy demanded a deep, unaided, quasi-gymnastic curtsy known as the "St. James bow." Abigail Adams, wife of the first American ambassador to the Court of St. James, participated in a formal presentation in June 1785 with some trepidation. She wore the prescribed costume of the day: an all-white dress with a three-yard train and the

This 2001 photo from a debut program could be of any ball, anywhere, any time.

ruffled cuffs signaling her status as a married woman. And nodding from the top of her coiffure were two white plumes that quavered piquantly as she bent her knee before the royal dais. For the redoubtable Mrs. Adams, it was she who had honored George III by her presence. In a letter home, she disavowed any personal stake in the fancy-dress folderol of the court. "Nor would I ever again set foot there if the etiquette of my country did not require it." Besides, she added, the Queen was fat and ugly in her purple gown.

AMERICANS LONG TO BE ROYALS

Yet creating a new etiquette tailored for a democracy proved equally trying. "Lady" Washington's presidential receptions in New York and

Philadelphia were patent duplicates of fat Queen Charlotte's drawing rooms, or afternoon levees, with Martha in court dress on a raised dais, inclining her head slightly to favored visitors. The first formal White House reception took place on New Year's Day, 1801. John Adams, sporting velvet knee britches and powdered hair, with Abigail at his side, aped the stiff customs of the English court for which she had earlier expressed disdain. Eschewing the honest American handshake, both Adamses bowed, just like the Washingtons before them. Some scholars have expressed surprise that the American etiquette manuals sold in huge numbers throughout the nineteenth century should have included instructions on how to manage oneself at a royal presentation. But the allure of all things British had a profound and lasting effect on how prominent Americans constructed their own social rituals, even in the White House.

Martin Van Buren's official White House hostess was his daughter-in-law Angelica, a protégée of Dolley Madison. While honeymooning in Europe, Angelica was presented to Queen Victoria, and she approved of the fact that Her Majesty did not shake hands, as Andrew Jackson and his rough-hewn supporters back home had done on all occasions. So, with Mrs. Madison's approval, Angelica built herself a dais and played at being America's crown princess, dressed all in white, carrying a beautiful bouquet of flowers, bobbing her head graciously, and flanked by the most handsome young ladies in the city to form a living picture of untouchable loveliness. At White House receptions Angelica stood on her little platform and, like Victoria, was every inch the aristocrat for whom a handshake simply would not do. Despite criticism of presidential airs, John Tyler's young second wife, Julia, the "Mrs. Presidentress," revived the dais and received guests in the East Room seated upon her little platform surrounded by a squadron of maids of honor. In their effort to find a dignified way to acknowledge the standing of the President as the primus inter pares, First Ladies and their surrogates were all too apt to make themselves into demi-queens. But their socially inclined subjects were just as prone to unseemly fits of royal worship.

Even ardent republicans went into a tizzy in 1860 when it was announced that the teenage Prince of Wales—Victoria's pleasure-loving son—was to dip south of the border with a retinue of British peers after a state visit to Canada. Officially, this was a private, hush-hush affair; in the United States, the future Edward VII would travel under the name of Baron Renfrew. But the ruse did not prevent New York City's elite from planning a splendid banquet at the Brevoort House. Baron Renfrew, however, had lost his relish for banquets and speeches in Canada. At the behest of the honored guest, who loved dancing and lively young ladies in equal measure, New York opted for a gala ball instead.

The arrival of the Prince was greeted with near hysteria. Businesses shut down for the day. Mobs of gawkers, 300,000 strong, followed the royal progress up Broadway to the Fifth Avenue Hotel. But the main event—the Prince's Ball, as it was ever afterward known—took place the following evening, October 12, at the Academy of Music. John Jacob Astor III and other worthies guarded the door to the supper room. Women of social position drove their husbands mad with demands that they petition the organizing committee so their daughters might have a chance to dance with Albert Edward. Visions of Cinderella and her prince glimmered before the eyes of Miss Mason, Miss Fannie Butler, Miss Fish, and the other lucky girls chosen to open the ball with a "quadrille d'honneur." Alas, the nineteen-year-old Prince returned home without an American bride. Perhaps, as a cheeky poet explained, Eddie had been after friskier game: "It was even said that his great delight / Established etiquette scorning / Would not only be to dance all night / But . . . to go home with the girls in the morning!"

To be sure, neither balls nor splendid White House receptions on the royal model were debutante parties, exactly, but they did constitute the instruction manual for the events whereby Americans would launch their daughters into high society in New York, St. Paul, Kansas City, and points west. And sometimes, elegant Washington affairs served as a substitute for at-home festivities, especially when the populace of a rural nation was spread thinly across the landscape. Such was the case of a Maryland belle—Miss Caroline Calvert—who was scheduled to make her debut in 1818, during the Monroe administration. She did so by attending the traditional New Year's Day reception in the East Room attired in a new wardrobe imported from Europe for the occasion. She then followed up her triumph by making the rounds of Washington dancing assemblies, teas, and the fortnightly ambassadorial parties of the French and British to which all persons of quality had standing invitations. After two such "seasons," Miss Calvert was still an "old maid,"

Alice Roosevelt, possibly the first White House debutante, in 1902. Although she professed to be unhappy with the event, she used this deb picture as the frontispiece for her 1933 autobiography.

by her own admission, but she and her doting mother had enjoyed themselves enormously. And Caroline's shyness had all but disappeared.

In later years, the White House also served as the background for parties meant specifically to serve as debuts. The most memorable was the first—the "coming out" of young Alice Roosevelt, daughter of the sitting President, in 1902. The affair was arranged by her stepmother, Edith, and the headstrong Alice chafed under her restrictions. The First Lady permitted dancing, for instance, but insisted on covering the floor with "crash," a sturdy fabric laid down to protect the carpets. Alice thought it was simply horrid. The color reminded her of "the underbelly of a fish." There was no cotillion, either, with cunning favors and flowers. And Edith flatly refused to serve champagne, the mother's milk of Manhattan and Newport debs of the day. "I enjoyed it moderately," Alice grudgingly conceded in the several pages of her memoirs devoted to the event.

Less critical was young Eleanor Roosevelt, niece and namesake of Mrs. Franklin D. Roosevelt, who came out at a White House reception and ball late in 1938. The belle had already undergone one debut in Boston: it was all "a racket," she observed, "but a pleasant one." This time, the debutante wore an old-fashioned gown—white organdy with a hoop skirt and many ruffles—perfect for dancing. Some of the numbers were modern: the Lambeth Walk and the "Eleanor Glide," devised for the evening's revels by one of Mrs. Roosevelt's friends. But some numbers were specimens of vintage Americana. The elder Eleanor Roosevelt, in beaded red chiffon, danced the Virginia Reel so energetically that she toppled over backward, according to the papers. Sly journalists also noted that white wine punch had been served in abundance.

In 1960, at an altogether more decorous affair, Mamie Eisenhower served champagne punch from a bubbling fountain in the State Dining Room in honor of her two debbing nieces. The five hundred guests were women in suits and hats. The decorations were pink. The girls, in long dresses, stood between Mrs. Eisenhower and their mother in the Green Room and were ceremoniously introduced to each guest. The Marine Band played show tunes and waltzes, but there was no dancing. The repast consisted of finger food—dainty sandwiches and cakes. It was the quintessential debutante tea, a starchy British-influenced reception plus champagne punch.

COMING OUT AT THE COURT OF ST. JAMES

The Eisenhower debut could have taken place in the 1890s, without changing a single detail. The ladies present all understood the ritual function of the afternoon's proceedings. By accepting the invitation, they were also accepting the deb or debs into their midst, as social postulants. In theory, one could have held a similar tea with a guest list made up of washerwomen or chorus girls (a group of famous music-hall actresses of the 1880s was known as "The Daly Débutantes"). But a debut is not a democratic institution. Unless the ladies—and sometimes, the gentlemen—present to welcome the deb are members of the elite social caste to which the family belongs or aspires, there is really no point to all the fuss. The tea is a public acknowledgment of a mutual pledge of fealty, cloaked in the costumes and customs of a regal past. So when recognized socialites could not be found to confirm the debutante's status in her own country, sterner measures were sometimes called for. In *A Hazard of New Fortunes*, published in 1889, novelist William Dean Howells describes the plight of the rejected aspirant forced into exile to achieve some measure of distinction. "Many American plutocrats must wait their apotheosis in Europe," he writes. Money alone cannot make the man, or launch his debutante offspring.

The back door to social acceptance was often the Court of St. James. British historians have argued that the 1880s marked the loosening of manners and morals in London's royal reception rooms. Court presentations increased dramatically. Thanks to the influence of the Prince of Wales—New York's erstwhile dancing guest—rich men of questionable social background began to appear regularly at such functions, with ambitious wives and daughters in tow. The old landed families from the countryside lost their influence, as brewers, industrialists, and merchants assumed control of the London season. Even the old Queen was caught up in the ascendance of the nouveaux riches.

During the last twenty years of Victoria's reign, the number of debutantes presented at her various levees doubled. When his mother gradually withdrew from such duties after the death of her husband, the Prince began to preside over the presentations, shaking hands, vetting invitees, and favoring, or so palace gossip had it, rich and amusing Americans. Just as the old British nobility was being elbowed aside by climbers from Manchester, Leeds, or the London suburbs, the number of wealthy Americans in London for the social season (May to July) also increased dramatically after the Civil War. There, the would-be patricians of the railroad or the stock market sought the recognition and acceptance they had failed to win back home.

As a rich young Canadian woman presented to King Edward and Queen Alexandra later remembered, it was "an expensive, exhausting ordeal." And a confusing process, too. The first hurdle was getting on the presentation list. The 1903 edition of the *White House Book of Etiquette* (Edith Roosevelt's is the frontispiece portrait) recommends finding a kind of chaperone or sponsor. There were, says the guidebook, "a certain number of titled women who hold themselves available as social stepping stones to young women" for a princely fee. Anthony Trollope's *The Way We Live Now* (1875), written shortly after his return from a trip to America, introduces a host of mercenary English ladies bent on extracting dollars from awkward colonials in return for vigorous press agentry. Those with political connections in Washington could, perhaps, avoid the scheming noblewomen by gaining the ear of the American ambassador. But the route that led to Fifth Avenue and Newport through the throne room of Buckingham Palace was a tortuous one, even for the well-connected.

First, the ambassador (or his wife) appealed the case to the Lord Chamberlain. Even then, an informal quota for American presentees made for stiff competition and encouraged more backdoor maneuvering for spots on the royal list. The fortunate candidates then immersed themselves in the mysteries of court dress. For New Yorkers, this meant a trip to Farquharson & Wheelock, on Fifty-seventh Street. That firm was rumored to have a direct pipeline into the palace and thus kept abreast of such crucial matters as the length of the train, the height of the neckline, and the style of sleeve permissible in any given season. Those without time for New York fittings were expected to turn up in London three weeks before their scheduled day of reckoning. With the summons card—the invitation—from the Chamberlain's office came an exacting set of instructions for one's dressmaker. At that office, one was also free to pore over sketches of approved costumes and examine the current edition of an instruction booklet entitled *Dress and Insignia Worn at His* [or *Her*] *Majesty's Court.*

The proud American Beauty joins the queue for her court presentation in this Charles Dana Gibson sketch.

When Elsie de Wolfe of New York, future interior decorator and virtual inventor of chintz upholstery, went to London "to look at the Queen" in the 1880s, she wore white satin trimmed in seed pearls with a long train, a tulle veil, and three pert little plumes in her hair. The latter stood for the Prince of Wales and, according to the official rules, were to be arranged around "a centre feather . . . being a little higher than the two side ones, to be worn slightly on the left side of the head" with a tulle veil—no longer than forty-five inches in length—attached to the base of the feathers. Gloves were a must. Trains could be no longer than two yards, or eighteen inches from the heel of the shoe. And, although the rules specifically allowed any color for the dresses and gloves of the debutantes, custom dictated that both single girls and married women wear pure snow white on their first court outing. Recent brides, in fact, usually wore their wedding dresses, as did Alice Roosevelt Longworth when she honeymooned abroad. The press back home played up the story of the First Daughter and her congressman-husband kowtowing to royalty, but Alice dismissed their court appearance as an example of the "slightly odd native ways" of the British. When in Rome, or London . . . ! "It seems a mere matter of good manners for guests to conform to the customs of their hosts."

Elsie de Wolfe, who was presented in May 1885, at the last "court" over which Victoria would preside in London, left a detailed account of the ordeal: the ministrations of an approved court hairdresser; the hours of lacing, pinning, and hooking; the crush of traffic en route to the palace; the debs, struggling with heavy trains, herded by ushers like so many well-dressed cattle into "the pens," or holding rooms on the long approach to their goal. Books, card tables, even snacks provided as the wait dragged on. Finally, the State Library, the jumping-off point. One last official check of her gilt-edged invitation. One last set of instructions whispered by a stern comptroller. One last adjustment to a cumbersome train, an errant plume—and off she went, her name announced in a booming voice by no lesser personage than the Lord Chamberlain himself. A tinkle of crystal chandeliers. A blur of medals and ribbons. A bow, somewhere between a tipsy bob and a dip. "And a little fat queen in a black dress" seated on her throne, with the Prince and Princess of Wales standing nearby. Then it was over.

On that Wednesday, 392 persons were presented at court, most of them women, many of them so-called buds making their official entry into society. Despite the rigors of a royal debut, not everyone was impressed, however. Edith Wharton, a member of one of New York's old Knickerbocker families, had come out at home, quite unobtrusively. Her mother bought her a gown with a white muslin skirt and a green brocade bodice, piled her hair on top of her head, and equipped her with a large bouquet of lilies of the valley. Then her parents escorted her to a ball at the home of a friend, where she suffered "a long, cold agony of shyness." But it was soon over, and she was "out" in the eyes of those who really counted. In later life, Wharton had nothing but scorn for the parvenus who bowed a knee to the Queen in order to achieve respectability on the upper reaches of Fifth Avenue. "And as for the American women who had themselves presented at the English Court," she purred, "—well, one only had to see with whom they associated at home!"

YOUNG GIRL'S EVENING DRESS.

Young girl's evening dress of nile green silk tarlatan over nile green taffeta.
Skirt plain. Decollete blouse has arrangement of large revers
with insertings of fine lace. Folded belt of mauve velvet.

EMILIA BOSSI.

Per

Florence.

According to the Marshall Field catalog for 1896, this was just the outfit for the opera, after the debutante's formal reception.

There were many ways in which a court debut for an American girl could be justified. After all, the custom was a venerable one, begun in 1616 when Pocahontas, daughter of an Indian chieftain, "came out" at the court of James I. And suddenly, in the long, sensuous twilight of the Edwardian era, everybody who was anybody trooped through the "pens" of Buckingham Palace in a cloud of soft feathers and rustling satins. American debutante-heiresses, such as Consuelo Vanderbilt, were coaxed into a "more generous display of neck and arms" to secure a position in the royal inner circle. Her wedding to the ninth Duke of Marlborough in 1895 at St. Thomas's on Fifth Avenue was arranged by her formidable mother as a dynastic union between American wealth and British tradition, a confirmation of the special relationship that kept Uncle Sam's daughters practicing their curtsies and fiddling with their plumes. The crowds that tried to force their way into the church and the reporters hidden in every nook and cranny showed how the spell of royalty or near-royalty affected the average American. The Vanderbilt wedding was the news story of the decade because it seemed to provide tangible proof that an American girl was worthy of the rank of duchess. That in a nominally classless society, in a raw, new country, the old European elite could nonetheless find its equals.

In 1957, the palace press secretary announced that "a deb can no longer apply to meet the Queen. In fact, there will be no debs. They are finished." By the order of Elizabeth II, presentation parties were to cease after the 1958 season. The annual Garden Parties would be a bit larger, but schools like Cygnet House, which charged £1,000 to turn pigtailed girls into debs, skilled in the niceties of court behavior, were doomed. Nor could aristocratic gentlewomen in reduced circumstances eke out their pensions with fees for social chaperonage of the awkward. Absent the "list," the little buds of springtime would have to make do with charity bazaars, the nightclub scene, fashion shows, the ballroom of the fashionable Berkeley Hotel—or a tatty tea in Grandmama's drawing room. The royals sometimes came to private balls, if the family was especially well-connected. Queen Elizabeth, Prince Philip, and Princess Margaret all showed up for a deb ball at Cliveden, country house of Lord Astor, in June 1957. In the late 1940s, at a grand debutante ball hosted by Lady Rothermere, Princess Margaret insisted on singing a medley of Cole Porter tunes, off-key, until she was heckled from the bandstand by a

Miss Anita Furness in gown and plumes: a formal debutante portrait by Haynes of St. Paul, 1896. Minnesota Historical Society

mystery man, later identified as the wildly iconoclastic painter Francis Bacon. One would scarcely want such a scene enacted in Buckingham Palace! The day of the royal deb was truly over.

Until the end of her life, the girl who had worn the proper dress and learned the proper curtsy kept her feathers tucked away in a secret place, among her precious souvenirs. In the days before debs had press agents, a lady of good family expected to find her name in the papers only three times: when she was born, when she was married, and when she was buried. But in their heart of hearts, many remembered an introduction to royalty as the pinnacle, the high moment, the summum bonum in an illustrious social career. A Minnesota socialite framed her autobiography around her presentation at the German court, where she later danced with the Crown Prince. One of her contemporaries boasted of having been the guest of honor at a similar function given by the Queen of Sweden in the early 1870s; she had also entertained members of the British royal family in her own St. Paul mansion in 1869. The exalted status of crowned heads in the United States was a subject for parody, too, among the plebians who mobbed princes, interrupted semi-royal weddings, and purchased photographic portraits of ballroom beauties for their scrapbooks. A New York concert saloon of the 1870s was called "Buckingham Palace," to attract the swells and lowlifes whose names were more likely to appear on a police blotter than on the society page.

CHARLES DANA GIBSON AND THE IDEAL AMERICAN GIRL

At the turn of the century, the debutantes whose pictures had begun to accompany newspaper stories of their ballroom triumphs started to look very much alike, thanks to illustrator Charles Dana Gibson, who defined and refined the type in the pages of *Life,* an important magazine of social satire. Gibson's earliest contributions to *Life,* beginning in 1890, centered on the status of the American girl as a pawn in the one-upmanship of the elite. New York's "400," his work argued, was auctioning off its debutantes to the aristocrat with the most exalted title (the cash dowry came entirely from the American side, of course). Gibson's double-page illustration for the Christmas issue of *Life* in 1890 pictured a haremful of debs in their white presentation gowns and feathers. A foreign gent with a crown and a monocle is dickering with

Uncle Sam over the quality of the goods. In later works, Gibson debutantes play the role of Christians in a Roman amphitheater, about to be devoured by the British lion.

Yet far from inciting the anger of the group he lampooned, Gibson's pictures made him into a social celebrity in his own right. Although he came from a family of modest means, he looked the part of a clubman—a Greek god with a mane of thick dark hair, charming, a dashing figure in white tie and tails. Gibson soon found himself consorting with the enemy on a regular basis. One night in 1894, while dining at Delmonico's with novelist Richard Harding Davis, Gibson met a beautiful young woman—the deb of debs—who so closely resembled his own creations that she might have walked straight out of his sketchbook. Her name was Irene Langhorne, and she was a Virginia belle, a so-called Southern heiress, recently taken up by Manhattan's "nobs."

In the Langhornes' circle of landowning friends, Vanderbilts and Astors were looked down upon, since they were descended from people in trade. The time-honored method for bringing out a true belle was to take her to White Sulphur Springs for the summer. If she were called upon to lead a ball, she became *the* belle of the hour, whose every habit, desire, and social appearance were greeted with rapt interest. May Handy, the Belle of the Springs until bested by Irene, had herself formally photographed seated on a throne with a sort of halo behind her head and a cool expression on her face, as though she were the Queen of the South. For Irene Langhorne, the round of balls, parties—her grandmother threw a "violet lunch" for the deb at which everything, from decorations to food, was purple—and sessions with photographers was exhausting but exciting. Even the *New York Times* was captivated by her "queenly" carriage on the dance floor and her twenty-inch waistline.

Thanks to the press, the teenage Irene was being discussed far from home as the embodiment of the gracious, mythical cavalier South. In 1893, Ward McAllister, Mrs. Astor's pet arbiter of social arrangements, wrote to the Langhornes, inviting Irene to lead off the Grand March at the annual Patriarchs' Ball, one of the most ultra-exclusive events on the social calendar. And so her father escorted her into Delmonico's ballroom to dance the night away with millionaires dressed up as archdukes and princes for the masquerade. From there, she made the rounds of every major debutante fete in the land, from the venerable Philadelphia

This 1905 gag photograph capitalizes on the craze for "Gibson Girls." Hulton Archive

Assembly to the New Orleans Mardi Gras, where she was named queen of one of the most prestigious make-believe courts. And so it went until 1894, when America's debutante—now the prettiest post-deb in the nation—met its most famous illustrator during a dinner in her honor at Delmonico's restaurant. The moment was electric. Edith Wharton once remarked upon the "almost pagan worship of physical beauty" at the time of her own adolescence. Irene and Dana, "Beauty and Genius," in the reporters' catchphrase: the two most ravishing creatures in the world were married in Richmond in 1895, with the bedazzled eyes of the nation upon them.

Of course, it was not long before observers reached the conclusion that Irene was the model for the Gibson Girl, who now amounted to a national icon. Proud, tall, with a long, slender neck topped off by a mass of shining hair, the Gibson Girl was the great American Beauty of her era, so popular that her likeness was printed on wallpaper and burned into wooden knickknacks. She was chaste, even icy in her girlish purity, athletic, independent, infinitely marriageable, desirable, sophisticated—a true aristocrat, a queen worthy of a throne room but equally comfortable on a beach or a golf course, at the opera or the Horse Show, or in a ballroom, dressed as a debutante par excellence. She proved the superiority of her breed. In real life, the flower of choice for the turn-of-the-century deb was the new "American Beauty" rose, huge, blood-red, showy, florid, and impossible to ignore. There was something of that rose in the female buds of whom fin de siècle Americans were so proud. The American Girl was a national treasure. Visitors from abroad were closely questioned about her, as if to confirm the superiority of domestic maidenhood by the applause of an older culture.

Despite rumors to the contrary, Irene Gibson was not her husband's model; the Gibson Girl had been created before Miss Irene Langhorne ever waltzed her first waltz at White Sulphur Springs. As she soon learned, debutantes with chaperones scurrying after them presented themselves regularly at her husband's studio in their white outfits, hoping to be identified with the artist's trademark motif. It was clear that Charles Dana Gibson was besotted with them, too. He drew debs alone in crowded ballrooms, braving the inspection of the envious. A portfolio of Gibson drawings distributed by *Collier's* in 1909 used a deb in white tulle as the frontispiece. *The Seven Ages of American Woman* (birth, girlhood, the debut, the wedding, the baby, aged wisdom, and death), a *Scribner's* pictorial feature from 1899, spotlighted the debut as the high point in the life of the Gibson Girl. But in 1896, Gibson took his first close-up look at the American Beauty abroad in a series of works depicting Irene's presentation at the Court of St. James.

By then, the Gibsons were minor-league plutocrats in their own right. One of his several magazine contracts paid $100,000 a year. And Irene's sister, the sharp-tongued Nancy, would soon, as Lady Astor, become the mistress of Cliveden. The ambassador had no trouble obtaining an invitation to the palace for the fashionable American couple. In depicting the momentous event, Gibson emphasized the height of the ceiling in one of the "pens," where gigantic portraits of royals loom over the ladies, arrayed below like a flock of nervously elegant birds. Mrs. Gibson and a companion, both in colored gowns, dominate the foreground,

ONCE MORE IN ENGLAND
At the Court of St. James' he meets his old friend Viola, Lady Fitzmaurice.

Charles Dana Gibson's satirical look at earnest Americans bent on achieving social prominence in the ballrooms of London, 1899.

as the younger debs in white twitter behind them. The matrons are in full flower—true American Beauties, beside whom the little buds pale. In a companion work, Mrs. Gibson sweeps out after the ceremony, through crowds of gravely attentive courtiers. But again, her elegance and stature reduce the nobles to mere window dressing. She always presents herself to the viewer in profile, with her chin held high and her gaze averted. One looks upon the American Beauty much as a cat may look on a queen. She is accessible only to the silent admiration of her subjects.

With his high-society credentials, Gibson was only the most illustrious member of a fraternity of illustrators fixated on the ideal American Girl. Publicity surrounding the young queens of the ballroom provided the inspiration for countless love stories about their adventures with rival belles and titled swains. Harrison Fisher, who came to be re-

Gibson's London *album of 1897 follows the adventures of his own wife at the Court of* St. James. *This is "Her First Glimpse of Royalty."*

garded as the nation's authority on feminine beauty, met the demand for corresponding pictures in the *Ladies' Home Journal, Woman's Home Companion,* and other mass-circulation journals of the early 1900s. Fisher was, at best, an insecure draftsman. His success depended on the lush color recently introduced by publishers and on his eye for the trappings of wealth and leisure. Although he protested that American Beauties lurked on every street corner, his belles breathed the refined air of drawing rooms and throne rooms. They went to college. They toured the capitals of Europe. They provided the model to which the working girl could aspire, the paragon whom the weary farm wife or the schoolteacher might well envy. His debutantes were the stuff of dreams, coweyed and seductive as they pulled up their long, long gloves while baring their rosy bosoms as much as Fisher's editors would allow.

AFTER PRESENTATION

"After Presentation," the beautiful Irene Gibson sweeps from the antechamber, chin held high, in typical Gibson Girl fashion.

The third member of the triumvirate of glamor was Howard Chandler Christy. Best remembered today for World War I posters luring recruits into uniform with titillating versions of the American Beauty wrapped in diaphanous flags, he is often accused of blatant jingoism for his pictorial insistence that she and her kind are racially superior to a brutish enemy. But even before Christy took up the overheated politics of war, he saw young women as the finest flowers of a distinctive American culture—savvy, fearless, and bursting with febrile energy. Christy was strictly a ladies' man, churning out deb-like American Girls by the yard for the periodical market and for popular books and prints issued under his name. *The American Girl* of 1906 includes a long chapter on the "débutante," she whose coming out ought to be called "the maiden's Fourth of July." These lovely creatures, the artist bubbles, are "the young

A seductive debutante created by Harrison Fisher for the "Girls' Number" of the Ladies' Home Journal, *1910.*

heiresses of all that is most precious in our civilization," a nation uniquely blessed by its respect for womanhood. "It is no wonder that our American debutante comes to her inheritance as a young princess is presented to her loyal subjects. What authority she has known has come from the law of love, not from the tyranny of manhood." The deb—the Girl, the Beauty, the Princess, the Queen—is the very essence of America.

Sadly, however, real American Beauties drop their crimson petals, and their perfume fades with time. For Mrs. Charles Dana Gibson, her later years were a race against the calendar. A sympathetic biographer calls her "the curator of her own monument" to the vanishing institutions she symbolized. Well into the 1920s, Irene haunted "Return of the Belle" parties (at which she always carried an American flag), Gibson Girl revivals, and the coming-out parties of her friends' children and grandchildren, as the senior grande dame. She still collected aging beaux. At the age of seventy-five, she called at the White House. Franklin Roosevelt's children, who had never heard of the Gibson Girl, were captivated by Irene's "charm of manner and beauty," wrote their mother in her daily newspaper column. But times had changed, and for the worse.

When questioned about how society had changed since the glorious night she had led the Grand March at the Patriarchs' Ball, or the magical afternoon she had worn three feathers to court, her reply was blunt. "In my life," she said, "I've seen the death of Society." What she meant, Irene explained, was that society had been replaced by notoriety, by celebrity. "We had what we called 'celebrities' too, but they were either people everyone knew anyway—people like my husband and . . . Edith Wharton. . . . Of course there were the others too, but one didn't have them for dinner. They came after dinner—to entertain." Actresses. Singers. Dancers. Even movie queens and Channel swimmers. None of whom had seen the inside of Buckingham Palace or worn the feathers or showed the vivid colors of the American Beauty to the envious royalty of the Old World.

etroit. December 1903. A debutante reception, in honor of Miss Alma L'Hommedieu, the second daughter of the family. Mama—as the mother of the deb was invariably known—wore a gown of black net, studded with jet beads. Standing by her side, Alma wore "a simple but charming gown of white tucked chiffon, exceedingly becoming," noted the society column in the next morning's *Free Press*. From 4 to 6 P.M. they stood there in the drawing room, greeting a steady file of callers, while female friends served punch in the parlor. In her left arm, Miss L'Hommedieu carried a dozen American Beauty roses, the favorite flower of the blossoming bud.

COMING OUT AT HOME

Accounts of similar afternoons dominated the social pages of the nation's newspapers in the late nineteenth and early twentieth centuries. Although a "coming out" at home was relatively inexpensive and discreetly private, the press paid close attention to such events. And there is no evidence that Mrs. L'Hommedieu and her fellow mamas needed much coaxing to provide the editors with detailed lists of attendees, servers, decorative schemes, dresses worn—and the number of costly American Beauty roses strewn across the scene. This was the fundamental dichotomy of the at-home reception: it was familial and homely, but it was also a highly publicized occasion for a display of wealth and breeding, if only in the verbal pyrotechnics lavished on every tiny detail.

The reception and the tea were pretty much of a piece: punch was a little more daring, perhaps, and orange pekoe a little more genteel. They were, in a way, Queen Victoria's courts, minus the Queen. Or rather, Mama and the bud took the place of royalty, as they stood there in what amounted to robes of state, embowered in roses, and graciously nodded

An American artist, Irving R. Wiles, depicts a "Russian Tea," c. 1896. Judging by the dress of the young hostess, this could be an old-fashioned at-home debutante tea. Smithsonian American Art Museum

to friends who certainly did not attend for the food (sparse) or the entertainment (at most, a tinkle of music in the background, from an orchestra tucked away behind the potted palms). They came for an occasion, a solemn ritual of introduction and acknowledgment. In the Victorian era, when the lives of young women were hemmed in by draconian rules governing their every interaction with the world outside the home, the guests came to witness a change of status, a loosening of the old restraints. Now, at least, the bud was free to move about in this circle of acquaintanceship. Mama was the guarantor of her ability to function in society, to exercise womanly self-control without further prodding. Mama caused the silver to be polished and the roses to be plucked as symbols of her daughter's coming of age.

The last edition of *Amy Vanderbilt's Everyday Etiquette,* revised in the 1970s and still in the bookstores today, treats the debutante tea as a peculiar regional rite, popular only "in certain places in the South." Such receptions are held by candlelight, even in broad daylight, the manual remarks. Artificial darkness seems to justify the fact that the chief participants are wearing formal gowns and carrying huge bouquets in the middle of the afternoon. An anthropological relic of a bygone era, the tea "sounds old-fashioned, but it is gracious and pretty." This condescending note is echoed by Cornelia Guest, self-styled "Deb of the Decade," in her 1986 debbing guidebook. "Poor Tabitha!" she cries rhetorically. Doomed to be honored with a tea at the home of Grandmama's best friend, age eighty-three. Little sandwiches. Ancient ladies with walkers and canes. "This obviously will not be an interesting social event," says Cornelia, a high school dropout who spent her debutante season of 1982 hanging out with trendy celebs like Andy Warhol and Truman Capote and singing at a trendy disco near Times Square.

Amy and Cornelia were wrong about the tea. In the 1960s, Detroit debutantes were still coming out at spring teas and receptions. These were rarely held anywhere but at home, unless the plan was to use the ceremonial introductions and greetings as a prelude to a tea dansant. Then it might be appropriate to move the festivities to a private club, with more spacious facilities. This was the true Detroit way, said Eleanor Breitmeyer, society editor for the *News* in 1964. No cotillions or assemblies here. No impersonal hotel ballrooms. Instead, private parties—modest or outrageously lavish—with the object of giving the deb the "extra dimension in poise and self confidence" that comes with planning and executing a perfect tea, with a bit of coaching from an exacting mama.

In the original edition of *Everyday Etiquette*, issued in 1905, the tea is said to mark the individual recognition of the debutante in the larger world: "Before this time she has been a person without social responsibility. . . . Now she stands for herself." Now she stands, at two or three o'clock in the afternoon, in full evening attire, carrying an armful of roses, and meeting people she has probably known all her life. In Rachel Buchanan's *A Debutante in Polite Society* (1888), each guest, passing the slender figure in white, utters a variation on the same formula: "You are a welcome and ornamental addition to our society." And she replies in kind. "Thanks, you are very kind to say so." The exchange is as sacred and inviolate as the canon of a Mass.

The tea was also the preferred method of bringing out a deb in San Francisco, where Christmas was the choice season for vetting the young. "Lady Teasle's Society Chat" for January 3, 1904, observes that local debs dominated the holidays with a variety of afternoon receptions, of which "mixed teas" on Saturdays were the most fun. This form of introduction was supposed to have seen its last days, the writer admits, but the prophecies were false. There is "no more convenient mode to make a debutante known to the friends of the family than by this old-fashioned method." Once the family bud had done her duty, of course, she then became eligible for hostess duty at every other reception in town: pouring tea and serving punch at such events demonstrated her newly acquired poise. And so the tea and the debut became synonymous terms. Old aunts threw teas in the debutante's honor. Debs had teas for one another. Not every tea was a formal debutante reception, but no significant tea was quite complete without a deb or two.

Some debutantes took the tea party as an opportunity to rest up for more demanding appearances at evening gatherings—at balls where they were expected to dance beautifully and charm every gentleman in sight, until breakfast was announced at 6 A.M. Others were bored to tears and showed it. A case in point was Miss Gertrude Dutton, a pretty West Coast deb of the early 1900s, who skipped out on her own tea to attend an automobile race, leaving poor Mama to face the throng alone. The society editor, called upon to fill her column with the number of

Life

From the "Debutante's Number" of the old Life *humor magazine, 1912: the bud learns the wicked art of flirtation.*

words owing to the Duttons' standing, was horrified but did her level best to shrug off the girl's obvious lack of manners. "No one can complain of a lack of cordiality in welcome," she argued, "nor can anyone who has ever been a debutante find it in her heart to hold a grudge against charming, merry little Miss Dutton." Deb teas, truth to tell, *were* a little dull.

But when approached in the proper spirit, when handled with punctilious attention to every nicety of etiquette, the tea was a model for proper social behavior. St. Paul railroad magnate James J. Hill, the richest man in Minnesota, had a deb-able daughter, Charlotte. In 1896, her mother brought her out to the cream of local society with a tea/reception for six hundred, held in the family mansion on Summit Avenue. Charlotte, in white mousseline de soie with touches of pink chiffon, stood in the drawing room between her mama and her sister-in-law, amid the usual American Beauty roses. In the adjacent dining room, women in "elegant gowns" poured tea. In the appended art gallery, an organ played softly, and a male duo offered a program of musical selections. Miss Charlotte dutifully stood her ground from four until six o'clock, "a young woman . . . gracefully fitted to adorn the circles she entered by right of personal charms and many accomplishments." Her coming out set the pattern for every other girl in Minnesota; it was the most important event of the week—and perhaps of the whole social season. The decorum of the Hill tea was the standard by which all subsequent social introductions would be judged.

In 1908, in the mansions of St. Paul, the tea was still de rigueur for debs. But debutantes were coming out into a different social set. Anne M'Kibben, a 1908 honoree described as "one of the year's offerings of little blonde, fluffy-haired buds," was introduced to "the smart folk of town"—not necessarily the oldest families or the richest or the womenfolk alone, but what passed for café society on Virginia and Summit Avenues. And all the debutantes who were recognized as such in the society pages had been invited to join her in a long, straggling receiving line. This was a formal tea, but formality had become a great deal less demanding. Looking back on the good old days of the 1880s twenty-five years later, the Minneapolis society page observed that the names of the events had not changed much since Miss Nellie Blakely had come out at a tea in her mother's home, a party attended by the social worthies of the day. But what the terms meant had undergone a subtle shift. Because the Blakely tea had been held on a holiday, for example, men had attended as well as women, creating a more lively atmosphere. Smart people, even then, were starting to be bored by stuffy gatherings from which men were excluded.

THE TEA TABLE: THE WOMAN'S POWER BASE

With some exceptions, the tea was women's business. They made and observed the complicated rules for writing and delivering invitations. They decorated themselves and their houses. On de Tocqueville's celebrated visit to America in 1831–1832, he became the first to remark on the prominent position of woman "in the best society"—this according to the redoubtable Mrs. Sherwood, writer of several definitive tracts on etiquette. Without political franchise, the American woman nonetheless wielded considerable power as the creator and sustainer of the multiple networks of social connectedness necessary to further her husband's business interests and to give her family a secure position of respect in the community. In the end, Mrs. Sherwood and her sisters had no doubt that this was the more difficult and important obligation of the marital partnership.

Men, on the contrary, were profoundly disconcerted by teas and receptions. In the 1830s, a young gentleman from New York described the tea as a physical ordeal, in which the guest was meant to juggle a cup of scalding liquid in one hand and a plateful of cakes in the other, all the while making witty conversation with the nearest overdressed, aged female. Flirtation was all but impossible under such conditions. Teas were often recommended by the rule-makers as the best way for a bachelor to repay a year's worth of social obligations. But without a sister or a mother to manage the affair, the prospect was daunting indeed.

The tea table was the distaff equivalent of the boardroom, and was just as formidable. Even the roses were dangerous. Paul Bourget, another French observer of the American scene, recorded his impressions in 1895 in a slender volume entitled *Outré-mer.* To his unprejudiced eye, the American Beauty rose and the American woman were very much alike:

so unnaturally long in the stem, so intensely red, so big, so enveloping, "so strongly perfumed that it does not seem like a natural flower." Such a hothouse bloom demanded public display. And so did the ladies he met in Newport, one of the social capitals of the nineteenth century, where women were always on dress parade, bejeweled and bedecked even in daylight hours with "diamonds as large as their finger-nails." There was something disturbingly excessive about American women, their roses, and their overblown social functions.

In the era of the Gibson Girl, the expensive, pampered American Beauty rose was as much a part of a debutante tea or a society ball as the bud herself. Named after the voluptuous actress Lillian Russell, the most photographed woman of her day, the American Beauty rose was also an important symbol in the elaborate language of flowers that evolved in the nineteenth century. It stood for affection, a polite way of saying sexuality. So the bud on display in a bed of blood-red roses was being advertised as a sexual being, a virgin decked out in purest white but ready for the mysterious delights of the marriage bed. Mama's little bud was about to burst into full, fragrant, enticing bloom.

The steps leading to a successful debutante tea were, on the contrary, exercises in restraint, self-control, and strict observance of protocol. What was the best time for a tea? Some guidebooks recommended five o'clock; others, four to seven. Saturdays were preferable, but only if eligible male company was desired. Men should not linger, in any case, but carry their hats with them and exit quickly. Ladies could leave their wraps in the hall but were not, under any circumstances, to remove their bonnets. Flowers, gaslight, candles, and music were necessities. The chosen hour should not infringe upon the guests' evening plans; for teas, formal dress was not required on the part of visitors, nor was dinner provided. How old should the rosebud be? The debutante could range in age from sixteen to twenty-two. Below that threshold, the deb was still a schoolgirl; above it, she was yesterday's news. If there were several daughters in the family, the eldest should come out first, even if this meant delaying the presentations of the others. As more and more young women began to attend college in the early twentieth century, the guidelines on age and education became more elastic and more accommodating of the academic year.

A plumed American Beauty by Harrison Fisher, 1911, from one of his many albums of pretty girls.

A bouquet of buds: the Bishop girls of New York City in a miniature commissioned by Peter Marié, c. 1895. Marié, an ancient bachelor, collected miniatures of the prettiest debutantes. The New-York Historical Society

RULES AND MORE RULES

The contents of the tea table allowed for a greater exercise of ingenuity. In 1897, the *Ladies' Home Journal* recommended a linen tea cloth, embroidered or trimmed with lace; buttered bread, cakes, sandwiches, and the like arranged on doilies; and a tea kettle, pot, and caddy, preferably in silver, with matching tongs, bowls, jugs, and the like. Sweets, salads, and ices were also appropriate. Even oysters. And up to a point, the style of one's dress was another matter of personal taste. The debutante had to wear white—something soft and simple and girlish, or the kind of dress she could never wear later in life with quite the same impact. A lightweight, diaphanous fabric, regardless of season: a wedding dress ready for the ceremony sure to follow the debut. And pearls, the usual gift from Mama. And, oh yes, a big bouquet of flowers—American Beauties were best—held in the left hand. Fathers could send these flowers, but the truly important deb received whole bunches of bouquets, which were hung on the wall behind her or fastened together with ribbons to form a giant loop worn over the left arm. If the deb was taken to the opera or to a dance after the tea, her trailing bouquets became visible proof of her newfound social success.

The most exacting part of the debut came long before the dress and the tea cakes were ordered, however. The diary of Huybertie Hamlin of Albany, who came out in New York City in 1891, tells a tale of unrelieved tension as mother and daughter struggle over the "invitation list," deciding who should be asked and who will be liable to come. In other words, whose acquaintance could do the deb the most good? Then came a round of calls in Mama's carriage. At every stop, the driver climbed down and delivered cards to the maid at the front door, while Huybertie and her mother peeked out from under the brims of their bonnets, trying to divine whether they would be received or not, depending on how the offerings were acknowledged.

The language of cards was more arcane than the language of flowers. Turning down the upper right-hand corner of an engraved card bearing her name meant that Mama had called in person. If the entire left side of the card was folded over, she had come to call on all the ladies of the house. And so forth. By 1890, such maneuvers were no longer quite fashionable, wrote Mrs. Logan in *The Home Manual,* but the custom persisted. Unless cards were received and calls exchanged, there was no official acquaintance. So sub-debs paid calls and left cards—properly mutilated—at the home of every potential guest. Debutantage was announced by the simple expedient of writing the bud's name on her mother's visiting card. But never, never were cards to be displayed like trophies of conquest, tucked under the frame of the mirror in the foyer!

The calls, the cards, were meant to alert the recipients to a forthcoming invitation. The latter was engraved and, in the best circles, said nothing at all about a debut. It was just a tea. In extreme cases of social discretion, Mama's card simply arrived by messenger, with her daughter's name written in below and the phrase, "Thursday afternoon." Matrons who knew their p's and q's were able to decipher the code instantly: "My daughter is coming out at a tea at my home from four to seven on Thursday next. Please do come!" If the cards arrived via the post, there was a special envelope etiquette, too: Mr. and Mrs. in one wrapper, all the daughters of the house in another, and every young gentleman in his very own envelope. Crests on stationery came in and out of vogue several times between the 1870s, when the tea was the preferred method of bringing out a daughter in the most elegant New York circles, and World War I, when such doings survived among old, exclusive Knickerbocker families, Boston Brahmins, the provincial aristocracy of the hinterlands, and the merely frugal.

"The conventional debutante's tea is a solemn and dreary occasion," one advice-giver freely admitted. The bud is constrained and subdued, in her gauze and pearls. Her deb friends are all but useless at keeping the party afloat. And Mama, unless she has ice water in her veins, is apprehensive about everything, from the guest list to the poor showing of American Beauty roses among the bouquets. It is a burdensome affair for all concerned. Father stays late at the office. Guests slip in for a half hour, sip some tea, and flutter away, bearing details of the neophyte's dress to five or six other identical events before dinnertime. Suddenly, Mama remembers that an important somebody has been left off the invitation list. Has her daughter made a lethal enemy out of sheer carelessness? As for the poor debutante, frozen in place and bored beyond measure, she sees her future unrolling before her, in a vision of teacups and tulle without end.

Even when they were allowed to attend, men hated teas. The he-man equivalent of the girlish tea was its mirror opposite—the stag dinner. Dining out at men-only affairs was not unusual. After 1870, as women began to show up regularly at public functions from which they had long been barred, men responded by creating more and more private affairs, to which wives and daughters were pointedly not invited. One odd example was the University Epicurean Club, founded in 1893 by millionaire New Yorkers for a peculiar form of dining: each member got a tankard of ale and a huge, broiled steak, the latter consumed in the manly way, without benefit of silverware. Other piggish clubs soon followed suit, as if to repudiate the petit fours and tulle of society as women chose to organize it.

The climax to these displays of testosterone came in 1896, at the so-called Seeley dinner, a stag party held in honor of a rich young man who was about to marry. His brother played host to twenty gentlemen gathered in a private dining room upstairs in Sherry's ultra-respectable restaurant. On the evening in question, as the thirteen-course dinner was still in progress, an informant slunk into a nearby police station claiming that "Little Egypt" had been hired to dance naked during the dessert course. When New York's finest burst into the room, the guests fled. The ensuing trial of the host (and reporters' interviews with the danseuse) made headline news across the country. The *St. Louis Post-Dispatch* used the story to indict the decadent East for the "nastiness and hypocrisy . . . of the so-called smart set" that dominated its own society pages—the cake-eaters, the operagoers, the rich, the haughty.

But the debutante tea was not as ghastly nor the men as carefully segregated as modern accounts of New York social life in the Gilded Age would suggest. The majority of debutante receptions also included coeducational trials of the bud's mettle. After the formalities of the afternoon, most families entertained at dinner for a select group of friends, including other debs and their escorts, with dancing to follow. When held in the home, this could be a "carpet dance" in the parlor, for which no elaborate preparations were required other than pushing the chairs back against the wall. If staged in a club or a restaurant, Saturday tea dancing often took place in a nearby room.

It was also traditional, when the season permitted, to cap off the day with an evening at the theater or the opera. As Edith Wharton tartly remarked, "one went [to the opera] chiefly if not solely for the pleasure of conversing with one's friends." In the 1890s, opening night at the Metropolitan Opera was a front-page item every November. Papers (and opera programs) printed maps that identified the owner of every box in the Golden Horseshoe, so that New Yorkers could participate in the game of identifying and ranking the personages in attendance. Into the boxes went debs in their white gowns, along with baskets of their bouquets. First-nighters in Box #3 in 1893 included a pretty miss in "white silk and lace" accompanied by many roses. The champagne flowed. The operagoers peered at one another instead of the stage. Diamonds were remarked upon. Young men slipped into boxes to pay their respects to buds. The lusciousness of the music—between 1873 and 1878, the old Academy of Music witnessed the American premieres of *Aida, Lohengrin, Die Walküre,* and the fiery *Carmen*—matched the heady atmosphere of the evening: the scent, the soft silks, the sparkle of jewels, the hint of romance.

Another favorite deb venue was the Horse Show, the event that marked the official kickoff of the "season." Debutantes and the blooded horses shown in mid-November had a great deal in common. One of Charles Dana Gibson's more acidic comments on the social mores of the 1890s came in a drawing of a haughty deb in virginal white. Her father, when asked by a friend if he is exhibiting anything at the Horse Show this year, points to his daughter. Whereas trotters had been much admired in the past, financiers and magnates went in for more exotic and expensive types, such as polo ponies. The ponies went through their paces, nostrils flaring, flanks quivering. And around the edge of the show ring was a promenade in which well-bred debutantes paraded, flushed, aquiver with excitement, weighed down by the bouquets that suggested their popularity and desirability.

Like the horses, they were there for public inspection. As if to acknowledge the fact, Alice Roosevelt even took her turn around the floor in a white deb gown shortly after her White House presentation. The Horse Show brought out a "brilliant assemblage" at New York's restaurants and hotels, too. The Waldorf-Astoria, site of the official Horse Show supper, was rife with under-the-table bribery as dames, debs, and anxious fathers bargained for seats at the centermost tables, the better to exhibit the young women to the world at large.

TO POUR—OR NOT TO POUR

The tea, and its various postscripts, maintained its popularity through the 1920s, although details changed over time. Modern debs sometimes dispensed with the white tulle dresses, for example. A Detroit deb of 1915 attended her tea in an apricot-colored gown with white fox trim; her mother was the one who wore white silk. Another bud, in 1929, picked a rust-brown chiffon number and carried yellow roses. Peach silk net. Pink with rhinestones. The old standards were slipping. Budget teas were also possible. When Nancy Davis, future wife of Ronald Reagan, was presented at a tea dance at Chicago's Casino Club in 1939, her mother borrowed the silver service and reused the yellow carnation centerpieces left over from the club's New Year's Eve party. The debutante was appropriately attired in white, with a single strand of pearls and an old-fashioned bouquet. But as soon as the receiving line had thinned out, young Nancy stepped up to the microphone and sang "Oh, You Crazy Moon"—badly—with the band. The day of the demure deb was almost over.

Nor was every deb keen to "come out." During the summer of her eighteenth year, Jacqueline Bouvier was slated to be brought out twice, once at home, at a tea, and then a second time in Newport, at the height of the summer season. The tea was bearable, she thought. But the reception, at the toney Clambake Club, was torture. She was introduced to stuffy old socialites she had never heard of, and she had to appear in the dreaded formal deb dress. Jackie expressed her reservations about the event by insisting on a $60 off-the-rack off-the-shoulder number instead of the Dior her mother preferred. She tolerated the white gloves to cover up the nicotine stains on her fingers. She carried the required red sweetheart roses.

But she hardly tasted the elaborate supper and instead retreated to the ladies' room to smoke with her little sister, Lee. Despite her evasions and scorn for the process, however, Igor Cassini, who wrote the syndicated "Cholly Knickerbocker" society column, named Jacqueline Bouvier his "No. 1 Deb of the Year," the first so titled since the infamous Brenda Frazier in the late 1930s. "She has poise, is soft-spoken and intelligent, everything the leading debutante should be," he wrote. "Her background is strictly 'Old Guard.' . . . You don't have to read a batch of press clippings to be aware of her qualities."

A SPECIAL EXHIBIT
"Are you exhibiting at the Horse Show this year?"
"Yes, I am sending my daughter."

A Gibson joke of 1898: after a girl's debut, the New York Horse Show was the best place to be seen by rivals and potential suitors.

One of Jackie Kennedy's many biographers calls her "a reluctant debutante." The phrase comes from the title of a two-act play published in London in 1955. A farce, a High Tory drawing-room comedy of manners filled with entrances and exits and mistaken identities, *The Reluctant Debutante* is about a bright young thing who doesn't want to be on the block in the marriage market—who wants no part "of the boring business." It was "all going to be a nuisance and no good could come of it," a production note remarks. Her parents, Jimmy and Sheila, soldier on anyway, for the sake of tradition, and everything comes out all right in the end.

In 1958, MGM gave the little play star treatment in a big-budget film directed by Vincente Minnelli, with show-stopping gowns by Balmain

Miss Jane Rogers, 1934 debutante. This photograph was intended for the society pages of the St. Paul Daily News. *Minnesota Historical Society*

and Helen Rose. The leads were British, but the juvenile parts were taken by Sandra Dee and John Saxon, teen heartthrobs meant to attract a young American audience. In the movie version, therefore, Miss Dee is the American daughter of Rex Harrison, and Kay Kendall the step-mother in charge of her London coming out during the last year of

John Saxon and Sandra Dee smooching in formal wear in The Reluctant Debutante, *1958. Wisconsin Center for Film and Theater Research, Wisconsin Historical Society*

Buckingham Palace receptions. Although the debbing here takes place at a series of private balls, the young woman relishes the after-hours sequels to the formal events. Cocktails. Pop music. A fresh crop of boys. To her, the nightclub represents both freedom and sophistication, or precisely what the old debutante rituals were meant to guard against.

In the film, Dee meets a most unsuitable young foreigner and falls desperately in love. The debutante of Edith Wharton's day would have paled to the color of her white tulle dress at the very thought of such goings-on. Hers was a sheltered, guided, and protected step into a society that was more like a family. No bounders or cads allowed! The tea won her the freedom to enter upon three years of relentless calling, card-leaving, balls, receptions, dinners, the theater, weddings, funerals, and décolletage at the opera. And when it was all over, there was to be an approved marriage between the deb and a man of her family's circle. If there was no wedding, she became one of the "leftovers." Henry James's Catherine Sloper is almost disinherited for promising her heart to a fortune hunter of whom her father disapproves. Wharton's Lily Bart, suddenly left without protectors after a stellar debut, fails to cope with the unspoken rules of society and commits suicide. Freedom was relative. Sophistication invited scandal. Ruin could begin with an errant glance during the last act of *Carmen*. The tea was a way of indicating that *this* little rosebud came from a family that meant to guard her in its bosom forever.

Stella Dallas, a sensational novel of the 1920s by Olive Higgins Prouty, ends with the announcement that Miss Laurel Dallas is to be "presented to New York Society at a tea given at the home of her parents on the afternoon of November the twenty-first, from four until seven-thirty o'clock." The rotogravures, meanwhile, printed her photograph often, observing that she "is one of the most popular debutantes of the season, etc., etc." But her real mother, the long-suffering Stella, must read about it in the papers, or stand outside the Dallas house in the pouring rain, watching the tea party through the window. A working-class woman, Stella has left Laurel's life so her father can give her all the advantages that a proper debut can guarantee. A radio serial, popular from the 1930s through the 1950s, harped upon this tale "of mother love and sacrifice," as the rough-hewn Stella struggled to regain the respect of little "Lollie," the society belle.

The newspapers in which poor Stella followed the social career of her daughter played a major role in the process of making an essentially private ritual into a public spectacle. For more than fifty years, the debutante tea—who poured, who wore what—was a staple of the society pages. Those mentioned in the lists of party givers and party goers also found their names linked by propinquity with Vanderbilts and Astors, whose doings were chronicled in adjacent columns of type. The social pages gave ordinary readers a sense of how the other half lived. In the 1930s, Chicago newspapers—all four of them—gave "the Season" the kind of coverage normally devoted to presidential addresses and acts of war. In smaller cities, teas were breathlessly described among recipes and sewing tips, but to much the same effect. The prose was formulaic: all the debs were pretty and demure, all the mamas gracious, all the decorations splendid. That, too, gave the reader the impression that the people being described breathed a different kind of air than mere mortals. Society pages helped turn debs into celebs.

When Archibald Gracie King moved his daughter's debut out of the family manse in 1870 and threw a ball in her honor instead, the tea was effectively doomed as a fashionable, upper-drawer rite of passage. In a public space—Delmonico's ballroom—the intimate, family-centered ritual became a grand, splendid show, with half of New York standing in the rain to see the Paris gowns and wealthy "nobs" described by the press. Little by little, the tea party faded into memory, unless revived for reasons of economy by mamas without access to ballrooms and unlimited stores of champagne. Debs no longer slipped out, by writing their names on Mama's card, or sailed out on a sea of lukewarm tea. Now dancing class became the bud's most important form of education, as she prepared to twirl into society at a debutante cotillion.

CHAPTER THREE *Having a Ball*
The Debutante Cotillion

ost writers on American social life in the late nineteenth century cannot resist describing the excesses of the rich with a kind of censorious glee: the multicourse banquets for which turtles, oysters, mountain sheep from the Rockies, and whole flocks of canvasback ducks gave up their lives; the summer houses at Newport, the mansions along Fifth Avenue, filled with spoils plucked from the stately homes of Europe; and, above all, the balls. Costume balls. Private balls. Public balls. Balls to bring out a debutante. In the winter of 1867, wrote white-tulle novelist and advice-giver Mrs. Ellet, "was introduced in New York the fashion of giving balls at Delmonico's rooms. . . . Balls for the 'coming out' of young ladies were given there; the proprietor furnishing attendants, music, flowers, and supper, at a certain price per guest." During the first season after the Civil War, six hundred more or less public balls were held in the city. Suitable dress for a woman attending one of these entertainments (with jewelry) cost $1,000, Ellet estimated. And that was a modest figure in an era when Worth of Paris charged about $2,500 for a rather ordinary ball gown. During the winter of 1865–1866 alone, dancing cost New Yorkers about $7 million.

THE DANCING DEBS OF NINETEENTH-CENTURY NEW YORK

Some of these balls were celebrated for their outrageous splendor. In 1867, Mrs. William Colford Schermerhorn gave a *bal costumé* or *bal paré* at which six hundred invited guests were told to impersonate members of the French court of Louis XV. Always ready with her abacus, Mrs. Ellet put the cost of fancy dress for that frolic at $50,000 a head. At a Fifth Avenue ball that year, fifteen hundred revelers rehearsed and

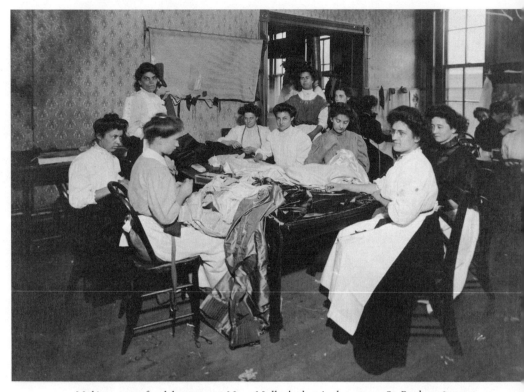

Making gowns for debutantes at Mary Malloy's shop in downtown St. Paul, c. 1890.
Minnesota Historical Society

danced a "german," or contredanse, dressed in costumes of the twelfth through the eighteenth centuries. In some parts of the nation—notably, Baltimore—a german was a ball. And a ball, according to an early edition of Emily Post's *Etiquette,* was a dance for more than fifty people (preferably a hundred, or hundreds) with at least two orchestras (to provide uninterrupted music), a supper, a smoking room, and both older people and sprigs on the guest list. A dance, in contrast, usually included only one age group, and only a modest number of those. If one could not afford a ball in good style, said the experts, "don't attempt it at all." Settle for a mere dance. Truly brilliant balls demanded crowds of fashionable people. Hostesses who tended to gather "all the oddly assorted frumps on the outskirts of society" were cautioned not to call the resulting mess a ball.

Not all balls were created equal. In 1893, a club composed of persons living in New York's Hell's Kitchen mounted a ball in the nearby Grand Opera House building. In the wee hours of the morning, when the strains of "Home Sweet Home" wafted through the ballroom and most of the patrons were gone, William H. "Flop" Dowling, wielding an ice pick, refused to leave, attacked the janitor, and was shot to death on the spot. This sort of thing did not happen at Delmonico's on Fifth Avenue at Fourteenth Street, where, lacking all precedent, Archibald Gracie King had introduced his daughter to society in 1870. Nonetheless, the King affair shook social New York to the soles of its dancing pumps. The mere idea of renting out his quarters for that purpose shocked Charles Delmonico, according to one of his confidantes; so cosseted were American women of good character in the nineteenth century that it would be another twenty years before mixed dining in public was acceptable. Society was shocked, too, when the invitations bearing Delmonico's address were hand-delivered. As late as 1884, Mrs. Sherwood, the reigning queen bee of American etiquette, was still undone by the thought of a young woman making her bow to society in a public place, however sumptuous the appointments of Mr. Delmonico's mirrored ballrooms and gilded supper rooms. "Now, do you not run great risks when you abandon your homes and bring out your girls at a hotel?" she asked, putting the words into the mouth of a horrified French woman of rank.

But soon everyone was flocking to Delmonico's to stage lavish events once held on a much smaller scale at home. The August Belmonts held a fancy dress ball there for their debutante daughter in 1875, with another elaborate kind of dance—a quadrille (loosely used as a synonym for a cotillion, or a german)—as the evening's featured attraction. It was said to be "more splendid than the one given the previous year in London by the Prince of Wales." Unless a father were prepared to add a ballroom to the family home, the public debut was the best solution to bringing out a young woman into a new world of social exuberance in which the old rules no longer pertained.

The Civil War was responsible for many of the changes that cast a pall over the genteel tea in Mama's parlor. Enormous fortunes were made by industrialists who had profited from the conflict. The oldest families of New York City, dating back to the colonial times of Washington Irving's Knickerbocker Dutch Manhattan, ceased to count for much unless the name was fortified with fresh infusions of wealth. Newcomers, including Belmont, a Jew, clamored for admission to the charmed circle of ladies who paid calls on one another. At the same time, a wave of nostalgia swept a city based on the rising and falling for tunes of the marketplace—a longing for the good old days before the war, when everybody who counted knew all the others, when every Southern maiden was a belle, and good manners prevailed. Finally, although Victorian culture has come to stand for a repressive Puritanism, it also stands for a love of material goods symbolized by Prince Albert's Crystal Palace Exhibition of 1851. Gorgeous fabrics. Jewels gleaming on the bosoms of the rich, thanks to imperial enterprise. Flowers collected from distant points by fast trains. Dresses from Paris. Lamb from the faraway Rocky Mountains. And immigrant servants to iron and polish, to sew and cook. For a sensuous age, sipping tea seemed all too ordinary. Americans could afford to rival the luxury of kings and queens.

Debutantes became dollar princesses whose dresses and peculiar rituals set them apart from other, lesser mortals. Music. The heady fragrance of flowers and cologne. Gaslight: the only proper way to see the soft gleam of the best silks and satins. Champagne. Supper at 3 A.M. Cotillions and quadrilles and germans. Costly keepsakes, or favors. Like so many enchanted Cinderellas, they set out in fluffy dresses to prove themselves at the ball, leaving tea-at-home debs to their frowsy, old-fashioned customs. The Cinderellas were the ones who made the headlines.

Cleveland Amory called the King affair the "point of no return," the moment when the private character of the debut disappeared forever. This was also the moment when New York society—and those who followed its lead—reorganized itself to acknowledge the postwar shift in power and wealth and the hunger of the press for celebrities whose lives fascinated readers. In his analysis of dime novels and working-class culture, Michael Denning posits that the aesthetic of the factory girl and the shop girl favored fairy tales over social realism. Everyday happenings were not worth reading about. But stories of fantastic wealth, unfamiliar settings, and strange ways of doing things were popular so long as the tale was set in the present day in a real city. Cinderella was the perfect tabloid heroine, if only she could wangle an invitation to the ball.

The gatekeeper of high society was Ward McAllister. Along with his patroness, Mrs. William Astor (his "Mystic Rose"), McAllister set out

Emily Post (née Emily Bruce Price), future arbiter of social graces, in a 1900 miniature by Carl and Fredricka Weidner. The New-York Historical Society

to balance wealth, birth, and style to create a coherent social hierarchy amid the scattered energies and ambitions of the 1870s. By 1888, when he told the *New York Times* that there were "only about four hundred people in fashionable New York Society," they had largely succeeded (despite the fact that his list contained only 273 names). The 400, he said, were "at ease in a ball room," which was the acid test of a socialite's mettle during McAllister's heyday.

Ward McAllister's real goal was to redefine the meaning of the term *gentleman.* In 1872, he persuaded a group of rich, youngish blue bloods to join him in an organization called the Patriarchs, which existed solely for the purpose of giving balls. The mere existence of the Patriarchs allayed Caroline Astor's fears about debuting her own daughter into a society composed of mannerly ladies and loutish men. It also served McAllister's interests. A Georgian by birth, he looked back fondly on the aristocracy of colonial times as the model for American deportment and noted the prevalence, in the eighteenth century, of organized dancing assemblies in cities south of New York, such as Baltimore and Philadelphia.

DANCING ASSEMBLIES: HOW TO MANAGE A QUADRILLE

Assemblies were clubs made up of inner-circle gentlemen who hosted periodic balls at which belles, not incidentally, made their first appearances in society. George Washington himself had danced at the Philadelphia Assembly, the oldest recurring ball in the United States, founded in 1748. The Bachelors Cotillon (the French spelling, very fancy indeed) of Baltimore, begun in 1797, held five germans a year; the prettiest debutantes of the season were invited to turn out in their finery at the ball held on the first Monday in December. In addition to a patina of history, the balls that McAllister envisioned were instruments of control. Made up, in the beginning, of Astors, Kings, and Schermerhorns, the Patriarchs defined the social circle in which it was acceptable for mamas, papas, and buds to move freely. The balls also allowed for prodigious displays of taste, elegance, and hard cash in the form of flowers, dresses, and diamonds. Yet they contained the sensuality of the event in a rigid form of social dancing—the cotillion—that invited few intimacies of bodily contact.

Alice Barber Stephens specialized in ballroom scenes for women's magazines. Stephens created this work for an 1895 issue of the Ladies' Home Journal, *which reprinted it in 1921.*

To teach the archaeological ins and outs of assembly dancing, McAllister formed subsidiary groups: his Family Circle Dancing Class met regularly at Delmonico's. The more arcane the rules of ballroom conduct, the "nicer" they seemed to his eager pupils, and Ward McAllister became a walking compendium of court etiquette of centuries past, heraldry, genealogy tables, and general fussiness. The man in the street called him the "world's greatest dude." To others he was a fop, Mrs. Astor's lapdog. Charles Dana Gibson caricatured him unmercifully as a goose girl rounding up her silly flock. People said that he did it all for the benefit of his homely daughter. How else could she ever hope to be one of the outstanding debs of her day? By the 1890s, his influence had waned, thanks to the publication of a fatuous memoir and a growing

Elaborate programs for the Philadelphia Charity Ball and other group debuts usually show last year's crop of escorts and debs. In 1976, the year of the national bicentennial, young men wore their hair as long as George Washington's.

realization that many of his dicta were simply stupid or mean (as when he advised New Yorkers bound for the 1893 World's Fair in Chicago to speak only to very rich midwesterners).

But these failings aside, McAllister left an indelible mark on bud-dom in America. Fathers took major roles in the process, even if their own "Mystic Roses" quietly managed the important details. Money counted: two orchestras, cases of French champagne, and spectacular dresses did not come cheap. And balls, even in the private enclaves of society, were really public events, witnessed by masses of guests, gate-crashing reporters, and the onlookers that swarmed the carriages of the guests. The debut became a performance piece. The exclusive dance lessons for young ladies, thinly disguised under the title of the Family Circle Dancing Class, made *debutante* a household word. A deb was a rich girl who danced. She was the one who "led out" the dancers, who "came out" when the orchestra struck up the first notes of the cotillion.

One of these odd, formal dances, in fact, put an end to the most bitter social feud of McAllister's era. With his help, Mrs. Astor had maintained her choke hold on New York society by fiat until 1883, when Alva Vanderbilt, a rich upstart, announced that she would inaugurate her Fifth Avenue mansion with a grand costume ball. Lanouette, the costumer, whipped up more than 150 gowns for the occasion, at $30,000 apiece; 140 dressmakers measured and stitched night and day for five weeks. As the evening approached, Mrs. Astor learned that her own daughter Carrie had organized a "Star Quadrille" to open the program and was rehearsing the intricate steps with her girlfriends right under Mama's nose, in the Astors' ballroom. But Mrs. Vanderbilt let it be known that Carrie would not be able to dance. Sadly, the Astors had never called on the Vanderbilts, so an invitation was out of the question. To spare her daughter's feelings, Mrs. Astor ordered her coach and drove in stony silence up Fifth Avenue, where her footman delivered a card to Mrs. Vanderbilt's butler. By the time she arrived home, the very last of the twelve hundred invitations to the Vanderbilt ball had already been delivered. The Vanderbilts were now bona fide members of the elite. And Carrie danced the Star Quadrille at their ball.

But what, exactly, is a quadrille? Or a german? Or a cotillion? Today, almost anything that involves social behavior is apt to be called a cotillion: classes in table manners, dances for children, a fancy dance that isn't a prom. In crossword puzzles, "person at a cotillion" is always a "d blank b." Even music experts have a hard time defining what went on when Carrie Astor and her coterie danced at Mrs. Vanderbilt's ball. Whatever they did was not strictly a new thing, however. In the 1850s, a series of "cotillion parties" was being advertised in what would someday become the city of Minneapolis, on the Minnesota frontier. At such events, a leader directed participants to form "sets" of couples, which meant that ladies were always at a premium in western outposts. The leader, the dance master, through a series of verbal commands or calls, then directed his set to perform a series of what were called "figures," or movements that constituted the cotillion. In the telling, it sounds rather like a square dance, and the opening positions did begin from square formations of dancers made up of varying numbers of couples. Even the courtly minuet was such a dance.

Contredanse, the French term for maneuvers like these, may have been translated into the American phrase "country dance." In any case, the kind of stepping and bowing and promenading movements that Henry Ford publicized in the 1920s under that terminology—his hoedowns— were a great deal like descriptions of dances done in Michigan in the 1840s, in Minnesota in the 1850s, at the famous St. Cecilia's Balls in Charleston in the 1860s and 1870s, and in New York high society thereafter. What all these dances had in common were great elaboration, considerable duration, and some requisite foreknowledge of what to do when the set was formed.

The Patriarchs helped to codify ancient rules of ballroom etiquette. Ladies were to be led gently through a figure or series of steps, never dragged along by the hand. Conversation ought to be kept to a minimum, so as not to interfere with the progress of the dance. Ladies must never be left to cross the expanse of the ballroom alone. Exclusive partnerships between ladies and gentlemen, even husbands and wives, were to be forgotten for the evening: the object of the cotillion was the general enjoyment of all. Mrs. Sherwood believed that germans or cotillions should always conclude a ball. The cotillion, she wrote, "is an allegory of society in its complicated and bewildering complications, its winding and unwinding of the tangled chain." "In giving the hand for the ladies' chain or any other figure," wrote another savant, "those dancing should wear a smile." Take care to grasp the hand gently but firmly. If the dance is a quadrille, instructed a third expert, "do not make any attempt to take steps. A quiet walk is all that is required." And "never hazard taking part . . . unless you know how to dance tolerably; for if you are a novice or but little skilled, you would bring disorder into the midst of pleasure." After all, order in the ballroom (as in life) was the best kind of pleasure.

Manuals intended to let everyman or everylady behave like a Fifth Avenue social animal defined such terms as the *pas marché* (or walking step), done in time to the music, and the sets of "four couples arranged so as to form a four-yard square, each couple facing inward, with the lady on the right." The promenade: "give right hands to partner and move in a circle to the right." And so forth. This was the basic square dance: the lancers, the quadrille, and the rest were variations on the theme, or preludes to the most advanced form of ballroom art—the cotillion. The cotillion was a game, more than a dance. The leader played, too, changing the music at will, encouraging high spirits on the part of the ladies and gentlemen cavorting with him. In a figure called "The Flags," for example, the leader gave a set of small banners to each lady, while his own partner gave another set to each gentleman. At every ceremonial bow, flags were exchanged until new couples were determined when a lady received a flag that matched her own. Cotillions involved props, sometimes chairs and costumes, skillful leadership, and lots of showmanship on the part of the dancers. Since the floor was cleared for their performance, the dancers were on display for the inspection of their rivals, their enemies, and their potential mates. Beauty, grace, and a little coquettishness were required to pass inspection by the hawk-eyed ancients seated around the dance floor. When a radiant Irene Langhorne led the cotillion at the Patriarch's Ball on the arm of Ward McAllister, she set a high standard of savoir faire for all future debutantes.

There were infinite numbers of figures in use in New York by the 1890s: the Cards, the Two Flowers, the Rope, the Mysterious Screen. The Hobby-Horse (also known as the Hobby-Horse Quadrille) was one of the most elaborate—and suggestive—with the men encased in horse costumes suspended from their shoulders and the women supplied with little whips. A Mother Goose Quadrille required the dancers to dress as nursery-rhyme characters, with appropriate livestock for props. Juliana Cutting, an 1890 bud who went on to become the doyenne of East Coast debuts during the Jazz Age, loved the old "figure dances," as she called them, for the skill and inventiveness of the leaders and the willingness of the debutantes to submit themselves to the discipline imposed by a program of demanding intricacies. The cotillion, to be sure, was at the opposite end of the spectrum from the free-form laxity of the Charleston and the Black Bottom. It stiffened the spine (whereas the underclasses slouched through life). A "means for acquiring the fine and graceful gait suitable for genteel walks of life," it prepared the debutante for her future, or so said the older instruction books. But Miss Cutting liked the favors best.

A detail from A. I. Keller's rendition of the Hobby-Horse Quadrille at the first cotillion of the new century. A Whitney gave the ball, and Harper's Weekly *covered it on January 4, 1900.*

After some ceremonial beginning—a Grand Right and Left, or a circle in which everyone eventually clasped hands with the entire company in a promenade—the cotillion began in earnest as a sport in which the object was to garner the greatest number of trinkets, ranging in price from a cheap tissue-paper crown to fancy gold boxes encrusted with real jewels. The young Emily Post, years before she began her career as an arbiter of social graces, acquired a certain measure of fame because, on the occasion of her own debut in 1892, four men were required to carry her cotillion favors to her carriage.

COTILLION FAVORS

In 1899, *Harper's Bazaar* unveiled the last word in favors for the upcoming season, warning hostesses that society dances succeeded or failed on the basis of the trinkets distributed during the cotillion. Although the editors insisted that cost was not the determining factor, the article praised the favors from Mrs. Cornelius Vanderbilt's cotillion the year before. These had been specially imported from abroad by a Mrs. K. J. Collins, whose business it was to dream up and procure novel kinds of favors themed to the particular figure being performed. During the first figure—begun at 11 P.M., before supper was served—came "shower-cascades" of artificial flowers and ribbons, which the men presented to the women, and boutonnieres of similar design that the ladies gave to the gentlemen. Clearly, under such an arrangement, popular girls might capture the lion's share of the favors. And how the distribution was handled also made a difference. Before the fourth figure at Mrs. Vanderbilt's gala, a giant gondola appeared in the ballroom, and a gondolier inside gave little Venetian lanterns hung on sticks to the women to light their way into the men's hearts. The men received silver hearts trimmed with roses, to attract the ladies. And so it went. For the final figure, there were tambourines for the women "to make merry the way home" and long, umbrella-handled cigarette holders for their companions.

Although some hostesses exhibited their favors on long tables, like the presents at a royal wedding, one did not need Venetian boatmen and gold lanterns to make a hit. *Harper's* suggested all manner of good-luck charms, wands, staffs, butterfly nets, big dice, hats or caps, Louis XV slippers, long German pipes, and the like. Or golf-themed items, such

The latest thing in cotillion favors, as recommended by Harper's Bazaar, *1899.*

as clubs trimmed with carnations. It was important to have somebody like Mrs. Collins on hand to send the favors to the ballroom in the proper order and to tell the leader which were intended for men and which for women. Servants could pass the favors on silver trays or distribute them from stands placed at key intervals around the floor. But memoirs written by ex-debs who danced in cotillions suggest that there was great variety in the gifts, the value placed on them, and how they were awarded.

Mrs. Winthrop Chandler, whose first experience with cotillions came in Rome, recalled the debut of Donna Clarice Orsini, where favors included beautiful scarves bearing the heraldic emblem of the family, and a servant disguised as a huge black bear, the totemic animal on the Orsini coat of arms, passed out bouquets of Parma violets, which each gentleman was supposed to present to the lady of his choice. But she also remembered partners who cannily secured chairs where favors tossed out among the dancers "would be likely to fall thickest." The most she ever managed to collect during a single figure was seventeen, she confessed. Other girls got more.

Young Alice Roosevelt bridled when her stepmother refused to stage a cotillion with costly favors for her White House debut. At the coming-out ball of Alice's friend, Jean Reid, daughter of the wealthy publisher of the *New York Tribune,* cotillion favors included velvet muffs trimmed in mink, silver vanity cases, and evening bags with gold mounts—and there were a dozen favor-bearing figures. At a cotillion held in honor of Marjorie Gould's engagement to Anthony Drexel in 1910, the wealth of the couple was emphasized by the costliness of favors made by a noted jeweler of real gold and precious stones. The extravagance of the Gould favors reduced even millionaires to mute admiration: competing balls began to dispense genuine, made-in-Paris hats and solid gold cigarette cases. Even Tiffany carried a line of favors. In New Orleans, practical debs began to attend balls with a gauzy sack attached to one wrist to bear away the booty.

This was the kind of detail that the "other half" loved to read about in the Sunday society pages, if only to confirm the vast inequities of income that doomed the urban poor to a life of misery while the 400 ate cake and took home bags full of golden plunder. The cotillion leaders, who stage-managed the whole gilt-edged business of wearing horse outfits and scrambling for favors, became celebrities in their own right. Mrs. Astor's favorite was Elisha Dyer Jr. Phoenix Ingraham, Worthington Whitehorse, Craig Wadsworth, and several other polysyllabic "society men" were almost as famous as the debutantes they put through their paces. Families hoping to emblazon their names in the *Social Register* (founded in 1887) sometimes tried to hire popular leaders to guarantee attendance at their cotillions, but these haughty stars could not be bought. By close association with a member of the blessed, they had purchased their own measure of social splendor. Such was Ward McAllister's bond with his Mystic Rose. Oddly, however, although McAllister's researches revived the cotillion as the apex of formal social activity, he was not a great leader. He was small and paunchy. He wore peculiar clothes—badly. But he did succeed in making the Hobby-Horse and the Mother Goose into ballroom standards.

Both of these were danced at Mrs. Vanderbilt's epochal ball of 1883. The Hobby-Horse Quadrille, performed to circus music, was no ordinary ballroom turn: the riders had practiced for weeks in scarlet hunting regalia made of satins and silks, and their horses were fashioned from genuine hides. In the Mother Goose Quadrille, a prominent society matron appeared as the title character, carrying a large, unruly goose. In the Dresden Quadrille, the dancers impersonated pieces of china. And in the Star Quadrille, Carrie Astor and her friends, in lovely pastel gowns, wove in and out of a maze of ribbons like orbiting moonbeams, forming a pattern of ever-changing stars. Years later, grandmothers looked back on the cotillions of their youth as magical nights and treasured their souvenirs. Edith Wharton's old Mrs. Peniston tells Lily Bart that, until her husband's death, "when it seemed unsuitable to have so many colored things about the house . . . I never threw away my cotillion favors. . . . I had a whole closet-full . . . and I can tell to this day what balls I got them at."

Henry James, on a rare visit to his homeland in 1906, used the quadrille as a metaphor for the childishness of American high society and its empty spectacles. It was, he said, "a great circle of brilliant and dowered debutantes and impatient youths, expert in the cotillion, waiting together for the first bars of some wonderful imminent dance music." The truly sophisticated socialite, wrote a blasé New Yorker in the same decade, was one who left the cotillion favors "untouched and disregarded upon the gilt chairs in the ballroom." But the cotillion has survived despite the scorn of the critics. It is no longer an activity suitable for any old dance. Now it is the distinguishing mark of a debutante ball.

DEBUTANTES, PORTRAITS, PARASOLS, AND CHRISTMAS CANDLES

At the venerable Terpsichorean Ball, where North Carolina debs are still presented en masse today, a figure performed by the girls precedes any general dancing. Called the "Debutante Figure," in 1949 it involved 131 young ladies, each one wearing a white dress and gloves and carrying a bouquet of red roses, forming a great wheel of extended ribbons around the Queen of the Ball. This ritual occurred between the introduction of each girl—and her escort—and the beginning of vigorous jitterbugging. New York's Debutante Cotillion and Christmas Ball (called "the Infirmary," after the charity receiving the ticket fees), begun in 1935, includes a variation on the old Star Quadrille, in which the girls dance a figure and then sink to the floor in a starlike arrangement to sing Christmas carols. In Chicago in 1957, thirty debs all in white began their charity ball with several cotillion figures. In the "Whirl of Ribbons and Bouquets," the buds twirled red and white parasols while forming the spokes of a wheel. Later, carrying lighted candles, they formed a Christmas tree. And, for the grand finale, the debutantes wove in and out under arched trellises of white flowers held aloft by their gentlemen friends. The rehearsals for the big night are no longer arduous. A recent California deb reports learning a simple figure dance at a special luncheon the day before her presentation.

Cotillions survive in a much attenuated form because they are traditional and peculiar—relics of an era before the follies of the rich were displaced from the headlines by the foibles of rock stars and movie queens. Besides debutantes and the Rockettes, who, in the twenty-first century, dances with ribbons and candles, making imaginary shapes on the floor? Like Mrs. Peniston's cotillion favors, the cotillion itself is a souvenir of another time, when a new social order was created out of tambourines, shimmering ball gowns, and live geese. The proper execution of a cotillion figure neatly separated the haves from the have-nots.

Eleanor Roosevelt's mother, Anna Hall, in a miniature by Katherine Arthur
Behenna, 1893. Mrs. Roosevelt later wrote that Peter Marié "called my mother a
queen, and bowed before her charm and beauty, and to her this was important."
The New-York Historical Society

Another fixture of cotillions in the era of Mrs. Astor and Mrs. Vanderbilt was Peter Marié, a rich old bachelor with somewhat specialized
hobbies. He collected fans and snuffboxes. He was a perpetual house-
guest and diner-out, a ballroom paragon welcome in the choicest of circles by virtue of his arch wit and his eye for the prettiest debs. His pas-
sion was a collection of more than three hundred miniature portraits of
the debutantes and belles who passed before his discerning eyes. With
gallantry and a sort of outdated grace, he wooed debs on the dance floor,

begging them to join his gallery of beauty. Some of the best painters on both sides of the Atlantic labored over the aged beau's quixotic project for two generations. It was, he believed, an important compendium of feminine beauty in all its infinite variety. And ever since, it has been traditional for debutantes to pose for portraits, photographs, and Papa's home video camera. The picture is as much a part of the cotillion as the ribbons and the parasol.

Although some debutantes then and now objected to the portraits and the cotillions—young Cornelia Guest likened dancing the figures to being on exhibit at the Horse Show—most managed to endure the curtsies, the silly fans and bouquets, the battery-powered candles, and sitting in a star-shaped pattern on the floor of the Grand Ballroom at the Waldorf-Astoria, trying to keep their white dresses clean. In fact, by the time the new century dawned, potential debs from every corner of the land were insisting on their very own deb balls, cotillions, and favors. Conservative Boston abandoned teas for balls and cotillions. In Detroit during the winter of 1904, Mrs. Henry Bourne Joy brought out her niece at a pink cotillion, so called because the decorations, favors, and most of the food were pink. The favors were displayed before the dancing began, and the *Free Press* listed the names of the prominent couples put in charge of their distribution. Under the direction of Ernest Baker, "the figures were original and pleasing and not too complicated." The scarf dance, the Maypole, and the peanut and cracker figures came off without a hitch; the latter "elicited much merriment." And the favors—walking sticks, baskets, tobacco pouches, gilt spoons, brass frogs, crepe muffs—were said to be "more elegant than ever before seen in Detroit."

Nor was this an isolated case. Minnesota went cotillion-mad during the early 1900s, with cotillions for debutantes, former debs, children's dance classes, and miscellaneous socialites. Although a bit of a novelty in 1896, when a group of bachelors formed a club in Minneapolis expressly for the purpose of holding figure dances, the members were soon searching out more and more difficult routines and better and better favors. The gilt butterflies, Dutch dolls, and miniature cigars of 1905 paled in comparison to the whistles, miniature banjos, and paper steins of 1908, when St. Paul's debutante assembly required two expert cotillion leaders to keep the affair on schedule. And the schedule of cotillions ran like a railroad timetable. Members of the receiving line, where the debutante stood between her parents, assembled at 10 P.M. Supper was served at midnight. The cotillion began an hour later and, if the dancers followed the leader as planned, concluded at 3 A.M.

It seems harmless, if a little strange, in retrospect. But contemporary observers of the cotillion detected signs of social decadence in these elaborate exercises in which men and women exchanged partners whenever the leader said so and exchanged gifts promiscuously with whoever was at hand when the music stopped. If the body is a medium of culture, then such doings simulated the decline of society, said one commentator. Now married women could eat at Delmonico's without their husbands. Debs could carry on as they pleased, flirting and flitting from one beau to another, in search of material treasure. Theodore Roosevelt, father of a high-spirited deb, charged the 400 with "rotten frivolity" and outright vice in a 1901 diatribe against the members of his own class who took cotillions too much to heart. "They are not serious people even when they are not immoral," he continued, "and thanks to the yellow press, and indeed to the newspapers generally, they exercise a very unwholesome influence in the community at large by the false and unworthy standards which they set up." It is no wonder, then, that Alice Roosevelt did not come out at a White House cotillion, exchanging favors with various "rotten" young dancing gentlemen.

By the time Emily Post looked back on the cotillions of her own youth, in 1922, they were becoming a thing of the past, except for group debuts, where figure dances reminded parents and older guests of the rituals of society in its glittering, golden age. Now, Post said, the "tinsel satin favors" are gone, along with the all-powerful leader, "a cross between . . . Lord Chesterfield and a traffic policeman." Balls had turned into mob scenes, with dancers crowding one another for an inch of space. When these same dancers were on show, performing a figure, they stood taller, bowed lower, and took care with their manners and deportment. The acid test of a well-brought-up young lady, in Ward McAllister's book, was her ability to cross a slippery ballroom gracefully. And in the old days, before deb and escort were literally joined at the hip in waltzes and fox-trots, not-so-pretty debs had a chance to dance because no swain was "stuck" with a girl for more than a few moments. But cotillion or no cotillion, the process of coming out had become a harrowing "ordeal by ballroom."

This may be the first dance organized by the Cotillion Club of St. Paul, Minnesota, in the 1890s. Minnesota Historical Society

In some respects, the survival of the ball and the cotillion was a minor miracle. During the financial depression of 1896, Mrs. Bradley Martin read about the plight of the poor in her morning paper and determined to do something about it. Her solution? Give the grandest costume ball ever witnessed. Twelve hundred "friends" were invited to the Waldorf-Astoria on the evening of February 10, 1897, to re-create a reception at the court of some Louis or another. Mrs. Bradley Martin, who planned to impersonate Queen Elizabeth I, let it be known that she would be wearing $50,000 worth of jewelry. But the costumes, the music (three bands instead of two), the food, and the decorations, she believed, would turn the New York economy around. Seamstresses alone would earn fabulous sums!

All over the city, Astors and Wadsworths and Cuttings and Vanderbilts were rehearsing their quadrilles, as were the season's debutantes. The quadrilles, in which a Vanderbilt deb appeared dressed as Pocahontas in

A belle in Eden: the deb as a figure of fun, from Life, *1912.*

a beaded number that cost ten years' wages for a whole family of tene-
ment garment workers, would be followed by a two-hour cotillion, with
even more pricey favors than usual. But instead of praise for her charity
work or the usual awed description of the wonders of her ball, Mrs.
Bradley Martin was roundly chastised for callous extravagance. Clergy

delivered sermons denouncing the selfishness of the rich. Death threats arrived at her home. Mobs gathered outside the Waldorf to heckle the attendees. So virulent were the protests that only seven hundred of the chosen dared to brave the sullen crowd to join the party. Even young Frederick Townsend Martin, the brother of the host, began to question this untimely display of "the power of wealth with its refinement and vulgarity." Oscar Hammerstein opened a burlesque at the Olympia Theater entitled "The Bradley-Radley Ball." College debating societies took up the morality of the affair. And the Bradley-Martins (now hyphenated) went into exile in Europe.

That should have been the end of balls and debutantes, favors, and rumors of reputed anarchists glowering outside the hotel as the dancers twirled within. Teddy Roosevelt, then the police commissioner of New York, ran into Mrs. Bradley Martin several days before the great event. She told him how pleased she was that the Roosevelts were coming. But they weren't, he replied. Mrs. Roosevelt was, because she already had her costume. But Theodore planned to be outside, with the cops and the Pinkertons, saving the partygoers from bomb-throwing maniacs unable to feed their children. In such dire circumstances, how could the rites of the very rich possibly survive?

CHAPTER FOUR

Trust-Fund Debs and Glamor Girls

Young Alice Roosevelt wanted a White House cotillion for her coming out in 1902. She didn't get one, but her notion of a suitable debut was in tune with the changing image of the institution in the early twentieth century. Receptions were passé. Teas were archaic. Dancing was a must, but a big, brash, showy dance, with or without figures—a ball so expensive and lush that readers of the society pages would swoon with astonishment.

The debbing business had entered a whole new phase best symbolized, perhaps, by the Mary Astor Paul ball of 1906. Cited whenever the culpable extravagance of the debutante scene was at issue, Philadelphia's "Butterfly Ball" was the event that marked the beginning of the deluxe debut. James Paul, the host, imported ten thousand live butterflies from Brazil especially for his daughter's party. Hidden in a ball of netting suspended from the ceiling, they were supposed to be released with a flourish at the climax of the festivities, much as the beautiful bud would spread her wings in society and soar after her gala debut. Alas for the metaphor, when the net bag was opened, thousands of dead insects rained down on the horrified merrymakers. The heat of the ballroom had killed the pretty captives. According to legend, only three butterflies escaped the gruesome shower of death.

THE TOP-DOLLAR DEBUT

But the little "accident" at the Paul ball did nothing to deter other fathers (and mothers, too) from spending grotesque sums in uninflated dollars on gimmicky debuts. Marjorie Gould's coming-out dance in 1909 cost an estimated $200,000, much of it for rare flowers, including "every American Beauty rose in the East." At the climax of Mildred Sherman's bow to twelve hundred members of New York society at

Sherry's, financed by her indulgent mama, a simulated swan exploded, catapulting ten thousand pink roses over the heads of the thunderstruck guests. Throughout the 1920s, after World War I had slowed the social merry-go-round momentarily, each debut became costlier and glitzier than the one before it. One papa paid Enrico Caruso $10,000 to sing a couple of numbers at his little girl's party. During a Newport debut, a flotilla of navy warships trained their searchlights on the lawn so that Alice Whitehouse and her friends could dance the night away. Natalie Coe's papa paid a princely sum to transform the Ritz ballroom, in Manhattan, into an exact replica of the family's plantation house in South Carolina. Real grass covered the dance floor. Real cedar trees arched over the corners of the room. The facade of the house, where the receiving line stood, was made of real red brick.

In New York alone, according to social historian Dixon Wecter, 250 debutantes came out every season, at a cost of $3 million to $5 million for champagne, rental, decorations, music, flowers, and service. Butterflies, bricks, monkeys, and the like were extra. The situation was the same elsewhere. Helen Lee Eames Doherty, stepdaughter of an oil millionaire, came out at the Mayflower Hotel in Washington in 1930; in honor of the occasion, she gave eleven Ford cars to her closest friends at the dinner preceding the ball. Helen had painted hunting scenes on the sides of the cars with her own dainty hands. The twelfth automobile from the even dozen went by ship to the King of Spain, who had been invited to the debut but had sent his profound regrets. Pundits who noticed breadlines forming up the block from the Mayflower were put in mind of Marie Antoinette (and her fatal cake).

But the rising cost of the debut was by no means the only change in the ritual. In 1928, Emily Post published a spoof on etiquette books for the debutante, with illustrations by the decade's most popular illustrator, John Held Jr. Held was to the 1920s what Gibson had been to the 1890s. His straight-up-and-down flappers, with their short skirts and bobbed hair, looked like crazed dandelions about to shed their fuzzy topknots. Free and loose in their relationships with "sheiks" in baggy trousers and raccoon coats, Held girls were in perpetual motion, too, excitable, energetic, and very much in charge of their own fun.

Mrs. Post presented this new version of the American Girl in the person of the fictional "Muriel," the ostensible author of *How to Behave*—

Though a Débutante. Muriel did not take her parents and her other well-meaning relatives very seriously. In her words, the "day of the wax-doll débutante that squeaked 'Ma-ma' if ever so lightly pressed is over!" Times had changed. In their mamas' day, debs merely had to waltz in competition with other amateurs. Now, debs had to turn up at chic supper clubs and converse fetchingly with Broadway stars, best-selling authors, and celebrities. They had to look their best at all times: you never knew when a photographer from one of the society magazines might turn up for a shot of madcap debs walking five abreast down Park Avenue after a giggly luncheon at Sherry's. Debs ran the show now. They knew how to cut men dead with an icy phrase, how to deal with crashers at their own balls, and how to wheedle exactly what they wanted by way of a debut out of their hopelessly old-fashioned parents. They were junior members of what was called "café society."

Café society, or the much-publicized high life that later became the jet set, was a New York City phenomenon, albeit the rest of the country was well informed about its members and its amusements. The term was coined by New York's leading society columnist, Maury Henry Biddle Paul, who was not one of *the* Philadelphia Pauls, nor one of *the* Biddles, either. Called "Mr. Bitch" by some, he was Cholly Knickerbocker to the nation, a professional gossip who, when dining downstairs at the Ritz one cold February evening in 1919, saw a group of people sitting down together at a nearby table. It was a mixed company of society swells, artsy types, and the merely famous, he said, "like a seafood cocktail, with everything from eels to striped bass." The next morning, he announced to the readers of Hearst's papers that old society was dead. Café society was born. Its luminaries, wrote Lucius Beebe, consisted of "four hundred professional celebrities, ranking from grand duchesses to courtiers, stage and screen characters, tavern keepers, debutantes, artists . . . and professional night club lushes."

In 1921, Paul developed parallel lists of the Old Guard and the new crème de la crème. Out with the elder Vanderbilts, the Shermans, the Morgans, and the Belmonts. In with the likes of Elsie de Wolfe, the Wanamakers, and the Whitehouses (of the naval Whitehouses, from Newport). Society pages had always been respectful in their treatment of Mrs. So-and-So's reception; her debutante daughter always appeared in a posed and carefully lit photo, framed in a gentle oval, in the Sunday

Brenda Duff Frazier, "Deb of the Year," 1938. This picture appeared on the cover of Life *even before her debutante ball, and Brenda became national news. The photograph helped to define café society. Bettmann/Corbis*

rotogravure. But the tabloids of the 1920s stationed themselves at nightclubs for unflattering candids, reported wild rumors as fact, used colorful slang, and spiced up tales of society on the loose with large measures of breathless innuendo. Cholly Knickerbocker was the spiritual father of Walter Winchell. The fraternity of New York gossipmongers created as their emblem of café society the high-society heroine—usually a deb.

In the 1930s, the flapper deb—the jazz baby—merged effortlessly with the "poor little rich girl" scenario. Would fortune bring happiness to the likes of Barbara Hutton or "Mimi" Baker or any of the Glamor Girls No. 1 who came and went during the Great Depression? Maybe their balls and their dresses weren't so wonderful after all. Maybe the middle-class shop girl and the young mother who struggled for economic survival were better off if they appreciated their loving families and the simple pleasures of life. As for "glamor," why, you could get a Ginger Rogers hat from the Sears catalog and the lipsticks of the stars at the five-and-dime! Haughty Morgans, du Ponts, and Drexels in pearl necklaces endorsed Pond's cold cream in the pages of the *Ladies' Home Journal* for cold cash: practically anybody could pluck glamor off the drugstore shelves for 29¢ a jar. At the movies, seventeen-year-old Judy Garland played a sleek New York deb to Mickey Rooney's lovesick rube in *Andy Hardy Meets Debutante* (1940): underneath the white tulle ball gown and the polished manners, Betsy Booth turns out to be warm and unpretentious, just like the girl next door.

The deb on the magazine cover used to be a generic figure by Harrison Fisher. Now she was a real live girl, photographed by a pesky roving reporter as she sipped cocktails at the Stork Club. Now she was Barbara Hutton or Brenda Frazier hobnobbing with Irving Berlin, the Astaires, Tallulah Bankhead, and Peter Arno, the socialite cartoonist who was also a graduate of the exclusive Hotchkiss School. Novelist Margaret Culkin Banning describes a typical day in the life of a deb in *Out in Society* (1939), as her heroine passes by a Fifth Avenue shop window decorated to show a day in the life of the glamor deb. After breakfast in bed and lunch at a fashionable watering hole, the deb/mannequin is seen sipping cocktails, at the theater, and, finally, at the "door of a night club, a rhinestone-edged slipper carefully visible under her long white coat," a cigarette in a long holder, and her "gang" already guzzling Dom Perignon.

Banning is most interested in the girls in thin coats, the women behind on their rent, and the men who have just lost their jobs, all standing transfixed before the store window, inspecting the scene where "the waxen debutante pretended to dine, her fluted ruby dress spread out around her." What were they looking for? Was it hope, or just a lovely dream in which the imagination selected "what they could not possibly possess?" And what of the parents of real-life debs? Were they worried, too—and determined to let their daughters dance away a fortune because it might be the last big party of their lives?

DEBS OF THE DEPRESSION ERA

It is one of the great ironies of American social history that the grandest of all debuts and the most celebrated of all debutantes dominated the headlines during the Great Depression. In June 1936, Barbara Field, daughter of Marshall Field, the Chicago merchant prince, came out at his Long Island estate with a forty-piece orchestra, a specially built outdoor ballroom draped in turquoise blue satin, and rivers of champagne sufficient "to drown twice as many" as the thousand guests present. Tables were painted to match the marquee. Turquoise blue lanterns hung from the trees. And the deb of the hour appeared in silver lamé.

Her sophisticated gown—unfluffy and defiantly un-bud-like—was in keeping with a recent trend toward the slinky, the shimmery, and the outré in coming-out attire selected by young women who did not imagine themselves to be shy little flowers about to be plucked from the bosom of their families. As early as 1913, a Chicago lass received in Nile green silk. A Minneapolis deb of 1916 chose a rose-colored gown. By the 1920s, bright colors in exotic combinations were the order of the day. Detroit deb dresses of the 1920s were every color but white: peach, with jade green slippers; orange chiffon; a flesh-colored chiffon embroidered with flowers shading from pinks to deepest purples; silver; salmon taffeta; "Alice" blue with a skirt formed of diamond-shaped petals descending to an irregular, gypsy hemline.

Miss Field of the silver frock had already met the society she had known since birth when her mother—now bitterly estranged and divorced from Marshall Field—decided to do it all over again at the Ritz-Carlton in a gold-and-silver motif. Five thousand gold and silver balloons. Gold decorations on the staircase. Silver-liveried doormen and waiters. Caviar and cake. A $50,000 bill. And that was a bargain price in the high-stakes game of debbing. Joan Peabody, whose stepfather inherited the remainder of the $50 million his grandfather had made on army food contracts during the Civil War, came out in Philadelphia at a $100,000 party in 1936. The Pommery (*good* champagne) flowed like

Mary C. Day, flapper queen of St. Louis. This was the heyday of sparkly gold and silver trim. Missouri Historical Society

water, but a surprise shower of soap bubbles that was supposed to have reflected the lights of the ballroom declined to bubble, whatever the cost.

Literary Digest tracked that season's debs from Philly and New York and Chicago to Baltimore, Atlanta, and San Francisco. The huge amounts spent and the bizarre decorative schemes (three hundred yards of white satin poufs here, artificial indoor lily ponds there) could be signs of the terminal decadence of American society. Or they might be signs of an imminent economic recovery. Quotable columnist West-brook Pegler called on Mussolini and Hitler to test their bombers on $50,000 deb parties. In Washington, D.C., four debs, deeply influenced by the New Deal, joined the impending class war and refused to come to their own parties.

The most controversial debut of the period was one of the first, that of Barbara Hutton, the fabulously wealthy Woolworth heiress, in 1930. By later standards, the four big-name bands (including the Meyer Davis and Howard Lanin orchestras), the forest of silver birch trees, the $3,000 worth of eucalyptus sprays, and the guest appearance by crooner Rudy Vallee—who did *not* sing "I Found a Million Dollar Baby in a Five and Ten Cent Store"—seem almost routine. But at the time, during the dismal year after the Wall Street collapse, spending $60,000 or more on a party seemed obscene. Nor did the publicity surrounding Barbara's evening present the debutante in a favorable light. Prohibition was still in force, but the champagne that Miss Hutton adored was poured without stint. Barbara herself was pudgy and gawky; given the attention lavished on her, the press clearly expected more.

One society writer, observing her lack of popularity at her own party, cattily noted that "You can't 'come out' unless you are going somewhere with someone." In the wave of fascinated disgust that greeted her too-expensive presentation, potential suitors stayed away in droves. Barbara fled to Europe, came out at court, and married and divorced a foreign "prince" with a doubtful title. None of these expensive diversions endeared her to the girl who ran the candy counter at the local Woolworth's for $10 a week. Barbara Hutton, Doris Duke, and the other big-money heiresses of the decade became living morality tales, "poor little rich girls" whose fortunes did not make them happy or even pretty. The headlines followed their every move with a ruthless cruelty, inviting readers to enjoy both the luxuries and the well-deserved miseries of the American debutante.

Just as movies with chic women in satin evening gowns and Manhattan apartments with Art Deco cocktail bars were palliatives for depression-scarred audiences, so stories of gorgeous, rich, unrepentant "celebutantes" (Walter Winchell's word) with tons of suitors also had a large following in the 1930s. The so-called Glamor Debs of the decade were excellent copy. Unlike poor chubby Barbara Hutton, Mimi Baker (1937), Cobina Wright Jr. (1939), and Brenda Duff Frazier (1938) fit the movie-star ideal of the 1930s to a tee. They were slim, vivid, polished. And they had been hobnobbing on the fringes of café society for years, perfecting their distinctive "debutante slouches" and bored, haughty expressions long before their redundant comings out.

Miss Mimi Baker, whose real name was Gloria, was already a fixture on the social scene by age fourteen, nightclubbing, gambling, and sipping cocktails. Her dark, shoulder-length hair showed up to dramatic advantage in black-and-white photographs in the papers. But shortly after her coming-out party, which was the usual bibulous, ostentatious affair for a thousand close friends, and her designation as America's first Glamor Girl No. 1, things began to sour. The *New York Mirror* ran an editorial charging that she was a decadent aristocrat, "not fit to be the wife of a truck driver." Her socialite mother, insisting that Mimi was "the most democratic person, bar none, I've ever known," was forced to defend her daughter's morals and politics to the press. Within the year, Mimi had married and thereafter lived a blameless life of upper-crust domesticity.

The public, it seems, enjoyed lively debs, but enjoyed them even more if tragedy and failure dogged their elegant footsteps. The elder Cobina Wright crowed that her deb daughter was the "most" girl of 1939: "Most photographed, most publicized, most sought after," thanks to a crafty mama who arranged for a screen test, tried to engineer a romance with Prince Philip, and spared no effort to keep Jr. in the newsreels. Nothing seemed to work, however. The new *Life* magazine disputed her Glamor Girl title for 1939 and named movie starlet Lana Turner instead of a deb. Besides, with the start of the war in Europe, even society columnists and determined mamas were shamed into restraint for the duration.

THE CASE OF MISS BRENDA FRAZIER

The ultimate Glamor Girl and the undisputed star of café society in the 1930s was Brenda Diana Duff Frazier. She came out in drop-dead white satin with appended ostrich plumes in 1938, just in time to avoid the social stringencies of World War II. E. J. Kahn Jr., who covered Brenda's debut ball for the sassy *New Yorker,* paid more attention to the reporters present than to the deb herself. By the time the last edition of the *News* went to press that night, Kahn wrote, "the whole story was ready in pictures—including Brenda being, so the caption read, kissed by an anonymous admirer. Reporters grew hysterical over the food, the music, and the cost (which was reported to have been as high as $60,000); and Elsa Maxwell complained subsequently that she hadn't been able to get a chicken sandwich." But who kissed Brenda? She insisted that it never happened. Her mother, meanwhile, in a statement printed in later editions, claimed that the ball cost "just under $16,000—which, as deb parties have gone, is neither little nor much." Whatever the price, the *New York Daily News* summed up Brenda Frazier's big night in a pithy headline: "Bow's a Wow."

Professional hobnobber Elsa Maxwell and celebrity photographer Horst hailed Brenda as one of the world's most glamorous women, at age seventeen. But the real test of her celebrity came at a charity ball sponsored by a consortium of fabric manufacturers in October 1938. At their Velvet Ball, she led the Grand March of the year's debutantes and starred in a figure dance called the Quadrille of the Coaches. The boys were the horses, with reins trailing from their formal coats. The girls were the drivers, snapping little whips—the favors. The other debs wore white frills and flounces. Brenda made her entrance in a simple, unadorned dress of pale pink satin, setting off a national craze for strapless gowns. A photo of Brenda looking pensive and a little nervous appeared on the cover of *Life* in November 1938: the pink strapless number was shown in enough detail to keep home seamstresses busy for the coming year. In the six-month period following the Velvet Ball, her mother found five thousand items about Brenda in papers and magazines and pasted them into huge green leather scrapbooks. Brenda didn't have a press agent, but her mother saw to it that she was out on the town every night, and most days, too, and the pile of clippings grew steadily.

Brenda's natural habitat was El Morocco or the Stork Club, rubbing elbows with the Duke of Windsor, Cary Grant, and Irving Berlin. A British journalist watched one of her head-turning entrances at the Stork Club. "As she passes my table, the other girls seem to become dowdy and passée," he wrote. When she was seated, she combed her hair, powdered her nose, and applied another streak of "liver red lipstick." Her looks were strange: the chalk-white face of a doll, quavering arcs of brows penciled over piercing black eyes, lank black hair with a pronounced widow's peak, and those thin, intensely red lips that looked coal black in all the pictures. Brenda was a caricature, a creature of artifice who might have been invented for the picture on the front page of the *New York Post*. Her expression was habitually blank, as though the wishes of her audience were to be inscribed on that alabaster face. "What Miss Brenda Frazier will do now that she is really out is an idea to toy with," teased the *Post*'s article on her debut. "The exquisite eighteen-year-old deb has been sitting up late in nightclubs for months. She has already accustomed her young and extremely beautiful face to a full set of cosmetics."

Babies and orchids were named after Brenda. She was "best dressed" and "most admired." Other girls copied her startling makeup (as did gay men at costume parties). The debutante suddenly became an all-American girl, thanks to a winning combination of money and a dramatic look that Hollywood's 1939 class of starlets was quick to copy. But it was Brenda's afterlife as a post-deb that sealed her fame. She was photographed from morning to night at all the fashionable watering holes: Sherman Billingsly, owner of the Stork Club, began offering debs lunch for $1 to attract Brenda and her pals—and the reporters who dogged their footsteps. Wearing an ocelot coat, she led a charity hayride down Broadway to Times Square at the request of the Coq Rouge. Her chauffeured limousine could often be found parked in front of the marquee at El Morocco at 5 A.M., when the dance band finally stopped playing out of sheer exhaustion.

Nightclubs gave Brenda free bottles of perfume and free drinks (she favored a ghastly mixture of Coca-Cola and milk!). On balloon nights, she competed with movie stars to grab the C-notes floating overhead. Chic Farmer, official photographer at the Stork Club, made his reputation on Brenda pictures that turned up almost daily in one or another of

New York's fourteen daily newspapers. The Frazier entourage included Peter Arno, with whom she was said to be in love, and the Irving Berlins. Irving, the nation's top songwriter, became a fixture of café society after his marriage to the wealthy Ellin Mackay, who wrote for the *New Yorker*. "Modern girls," she stated in a commentary on the cabaret scene, "are conscious of the importance of their own identity." But what, exactly, was Brenda Frazier's "identity"? What was her claim to fame, her particular talent—except being a teenager fixated on redoing her lipstick? Brenda Frazier was among the first of a new breed of celebrities famous simply for being famous.

When she set sail for a Nassau vacation, there were pictures of a windswept Brenda bundled up in furs. When Mickey Rooney came to town to promote *Andy Hardy Meets Debutante*, the studio arranged for him to dine with the genuine article—Miss Brenda "Glamor Girl" Frazier—and to be photographed while doing so. The young Bill Holden, in New York on a promotional tour of his own, ended his evening at Brenda's ringside table at the Stork Club. When Arno walked in with another girl on his arm, Brenda stalked out, assuring Holden of headline coverage. In 1963, in a confessional article for *Life*, Brenda Frazier called her debut season "a horror," a symbol "of the hollowness of so much of American . . . social life." At seventeen, she said, her mother had pushed her into the limelight, against her will: "I was a fad that year, the way midget golf was once a fad, or flagpole sitting." And she hated every glamorous minute of it. A poem supposedly scribbled by Brenda on a cocktail napkin during another boring night at ringside summed up her grievances: "I give the impression of savoir-faire, / Everyone I meet gives me an inward scare. / . . . I grit my teeth and smile at my enemies, / I sit at the Stork Club and talk to nonentities."

In fact, after an overdose of Brenda Frazier, crowds sometimes booed when she made her entrance. Editorial writers used the frivolous Brenda as a scapegoat for whatever was wrong with "the system." *Scribner's* ran a paragraph observing that Miss Frazier had not actually graduated from any of the various finishing schools in which she polished her manners. But Brenda was, nonetheless, the most publicized adolescent in the land: "She is now seventeen years old, has $8,000,000 in her own name." The *New Republic* did a financial analysis of her trust fund, on deposit at the Chase Manhattan Bank, and offered mock condolences to a child so deprived that her trustees balked at the pittance spent on her debut. "Most of all," complained an Iowa paper, "we're tired of pictures of Brenda Duff Frazier. We've seen Brenda Duff being the No. 1 debutante. We've seen her being a home girl, a play girl, a glamor girl—in fact every type of girl except perhaps the girl friend of the whirling dervish. . . . Maybe she's tired of pictures of Brenda Duff Frazier, too."

Maybe café society was tired of debutantes. In December 1938, during Brenda Frazier's coming-out season, a group of men-about-town staged a phony debut at Chez Fire House. The supposed deb, daughter of a barge captain, made her living as a model, posing for fashion shots. Her fourteen "uncles," including Peter Arno, Lucius Beebe, George Balanchine, and sculptor Isamu Noguchi, stood in a formal receiving line to greet Gloria Swanson, Madeline Carroll, Mark Hanna, and a host of lesser lights. At the end of the party, Miss Wilma Bard let it be known that, having just come out in style, she had decided to go right back in again. The *New York Post* featured the event on the society page, among legitimate notices of luncheons and the comings and goings of bona fide notables. The parody signaled that even those who helped make debutantes into celebrities had reservations about doing so. In the cold December of 1938, should anyone be lauded simply for having a debutante ball and then nightclubbing her life away—as factories closed, crops failed, and mortgages were foreclosed upon?

The anti-deb backlash inspired a perverse career mania among the trust-fund buds of the 1930s. Brenda Frazier, for example, appeared in a number of magazine ads, including one for the Studebaker Land Cruiser. Copywriters showed themselves attuned to the dual nature of the social butterfly as paragon and, in some circles, parasite. On the one hand, it was easy to believe that Miss Frazier would drive such an elegant vehicle and would observe approvingly that it had been styled by the famous industrial designer Raymond Loewy. On the other hand, she is described in a vignette as "born to the purple but charmingly democratic," a deb "whose honesty and graciousness have become an American legend." So her eye for glamor and her good manners became selling points for a car intended for "the smart younger set." Brenda wanna-bes and habitual readers of society columns were potential candidates for Studebaker's easy credit terms. During Brenda's run as society's darling, she was asked to endorse any number of products,

"Driving my new Studebaker is really thrilling"

says popular young socialite

MISS *Brenda Frazier*

"It's such an alive motor car," says Miss Frazier. "It's so responsive to the touch and it's finished and styled so smartly! Raymond Loewy, who had a hand in designing it, certainly is to be complimented."

ONE look at the smooth, sweeping, impressive lines and flawless appointments of this new Studebaker Land Cruiser and you understand why it's such a favorite with the smart younger set.

Possibly no new car of the year has won such extensive and enthusiastic social approval as this roomy, restful-riding Studebaker Land Cruiser. And it's one of the most money-saving of all cars to operate.

You can count on Studebaker's unique master craftsmanship to keep this distinctive Land Cruiser running smoothly and satisfactorily for many years.

See it and drive it now at your local Studebaker dealer's. Use your present car as part payment—easy C.I.T. terms.

BORN TO THE PURPLE BUT CHARMINGLY DEMOCRATIC is young Miss Brenda Frazier whose beauty and graciousness have become an American legend. This popular young woman proudly and competently drives her new Studebaker Land Cruiser many hundreds of miles each month.

Distinctively smart new **STUDEBAKER LAND CRUISER**
AVAILABLE ON COMMANDER SIX OR PRESIDENT EIGHT CHASSIS

Brenda Frazier, super-deb of the 1930s, lends class to the Studebaker in this 1938 ad by recommending Raymond Loewy's innovative design for the car.

Debutantes endorse cigarettes in the pages of Vogue, 1940. *These are the prominent Beadleston sisters of New York and Long Island.*

including a line of "Brenda linens." Posing for ads "was silly but fun," she remembered. "I found it amusing that I should be paid to recommend a particular make of car—I who had never been permitted to drive an automobile and went everywhere by . . . chauffeured limousine."

There is some disagreement over which deb cashed in on her class first. Some historians pump for Mary Taylor, who endorsed cigarettes and cosmetics and modeled clothes for exclusive Gotham dress shops. Others say that Mrs. W. K. Vanderbilt—or was it Miss Anne Morgan?—opened the floodgates by appearing in an advertisement for a Simmons mattress, for $5,000. Pond's cold cream paid its society women the same amount. Cigarette ads were worth $3,000, unless it was a group ad; in that case, each socialite got $50. Other companies paid debs and dowagers in kind. The preferred "career" for debs, however, was that of nightclub singer. In the early 1930s, such girls, said Cleveland Amory, "provided the opening number chorus for the Glamor Girls to follow." In 1935, an actual chorus of six perky debs and post-debs headed the bill at the Starlight Roof, high above the Waldorf. Cobina Sr. and Jr. both hit the nightclub circuit, as did Eve Symington, Gay Adams, and Princess Laura Rospigliosi. One of Margaret Banning's debutante/heroines aspires to be a nightclub singer with a coast-to-coast radio hookup. To the dismay of her parents, young Barbara gets a temporary job at the "Moth Club," but the applause is sparse. "There's a debutante in half the shows in New York now," complains one patron, "and are they terrible or are they not? . . . No personality, most of them. Cute clotheshorses, that's all."

In *Mansfield Park,* Jane Austen has her protagonists speculate about whether a young woman of their acquaintance is "out" or not. She has never been to a ball, so the matter is very much in doubt. In the 1920s, 1930s, and early 1940s in America, no such questions arose. You were "out" if you had a ball of your own, your picture in the papers, a date every night thereafter, free lunches, and endorsement contracts. Old-fashioned girls used to call Sherry's restaurant the "Debutante's Heaven." Glamor Girls nibbled chicken salads at El Morocco. Or, like Miss Valerie Axtell of the Nashville Axtells—a recent debutante—appeared in a *Saturday Evening Post* ad for Maxwell House Coffee, representing the taste of the gracious Old South. They smoked for the camera, like Lucy Carver Williams of Boston, whose craving for Camels legitimated a habit once forbidden to women. They went to parties for

Among the Society Debutantes of Eleven Cities

this soap leads all others in popularity for the care of the skin

YOUNG society girls of eleven cities, asked what soap they use for their skin, replied overwhelmingly, "Woodbury's Facial Soap!"

From luxurious, jazz-loving New York to strait-laced Philadelphia—from Boston, aristocratic and high-brow, to lovely romantic Baltimore, Nashville, New Orleans—the answer was the same.

"Life-giving"—"marvelous for the skin," say New York debutantes

In New York, Woodbury's was nearly three times as popular among society debutantes as any other toilet soap.

Among the lovely debutantes of Southern cities—Baltimore—Nashville—New Orleans—Savannah—Birmingham—Richmond—Atlanta—Woodbury's was nine times as popular.

In conservative Philadelphia, Woodbury's was preferred seven times to any other.

Two-thirds of Boston debutantes were using Woodbury's; more than half the Washington debutantes.

"Its purity" was the quality they named oftenest, in telling why they prefer Woodbury's. "Its soothing non-irritating effect on the skin."

A SKIN SPECIALIST worked out the formula by which Woodbury's Facial Soap is made. This formula not only calls for the purest and finest ingredients; it also demands greater refinement in the manufacturing process than is commercially possible with ordinary soap.

A 25-cent cake of Woodbury's lasts a month or six weeks. Around each cake is wrapped a booklet of famous skin treatments for overcoming common skin

defects. Within a week or ten days after beginning to use Woodbury's, you will notice an improvement in your complexion. Get a cake to-day—begin to-night the treatment your skin needs?

That last lingering look in the mirror—does it show a skin radiant with fresh beauty?

Send today for the large-size Trial Set!

The Andrew Jergens Co., 1807 Alfred Street, Cincinnati, Ohio.

Fill the enclosed 10c please send me the new large-size trial cake of Woodbury's Facial Soap, the Cold Cream, Facial Cream and Powder, and the treatment booklet, "A Skin You Love to Touch." If you live in Canada, address The Andrew Jergens Co., Limited, 1807 Sherbrooke Street, Perth, Ont.

Name ....

Street ....

City .... State ....

Copyright, 1927, by The Andrew Jergens Co.

Debutantes from eleven cities all approve of soap, Ladies' Home Journal, *1927.*

A Southern deb sells coffee in the Saturday Evening Post, *1941. Illustrator Henry Raleigh, who specialized in genteel social atmospherics, had worked for Maxwell House since the 1920s.*

their kind thrown by *Vogue*'s publisher and, as often as not, wound up in its pages, lending glamor to the latest designer fashions. Young Julia Gardiner, the debutante who married the President of the United States in 1844, had once been known as the "Rose of Long Island," and her likeness sold a dress line in the ads of her day. Was there any significant difference among the deeds of the Misses Gardiner, Axtell, Williams, and Frazier, all of whom did nothing but become famous?

Henry Luce, founder and publisher of several of the most widely read American magazines of the twentieth century, was obsessed with debutantes and class. In March 1923, when *Time* was unveiled, he recruited that year's crop of New York debs to run the circulation department. By some accounts, the girls treated their "jobs" as a lark, another publicity stunt comparable to a debutante hayride or the Philadelphia deb "safari" organized in the mid-1930s to boost attendance at the Fairmont Park Zoo. The first issue of *Time* was almost its last: some subscribers got four or five copies, while others got none. But Luce used the debs because he initially intended his magazines for the upper crust. Even Luce's *Life*, the quintessential mass-market picture journal, regularly ran features on debutante balls, debs, and the doings of high society.

The articles confirmed the image of the madcap deb, the darling of the nightclub set. F. Scott Fitzgerald's one-act play "The Debutante" (later incorporated into *This Side of Paradise*) was a brittle comedy about courtship under the new dispensation of café society. Unable to find her daughter at a crucial moment, an irate mama throws up her hands in mock defeat: "For all I know she may be at the Cocoanut Grove with some football player on the night of her debut." And all this after her father has "marshalled eight bachelor millionaires to meet her." Clare Boothe Luce's satirical comedy *The Women* (1936) features a similar scene in which a dowager and her debutante daughter square off in the powder room of Manhattan night spot over the latter's penchant for wild dancing, champagne guzzling, and making eyes at total strangers. The debutante had become a type: flighty, arch, beautifully dressed, and irresponsible.

If the modern deb in the green coming-out dress did not succeed as a magazine executive, at least she had the satisfaction of knowing that she contributed to the economy in other ways. "We helped to give employment during the depression," says one fictional deb to another in a 1932 spoof on the social benefits of coming out. The dress, the whiskey, the food, and the imported cigarettes all cost a bundle. And so did repairs to the premises, trampled by the drunken prep-school boys who had been invited because their names appeared on a "list" sold to the families of prospective debutantes by Juliana Cutting and the other mercenary misses who ran agencies to run debuts. As early as the 1920s, parents had begun to complain that they were spending vast sums for the entertainment of tipsy schoolboys and aging athletes who were in no position to marry their daughters. The bare minimum was $25,000 for the multiple orchestras, the caterer, the decorator, and the damnable list. And all for what? To provide jobs for indigent bartenders? So Zoe or Mimi or Peaches could sing at the Club Boom Boom? Or mix up the subscription forms at Mr. Luce's office?

POSTWAR EXTRAVAGANZAS

World War II called a temporary halt to the revels. Nightclubs closed their doors. Debutantes kept low profiles. The postwar scene revolved around group debuts staged on behalf of charitable causes, which gave the illusion of being more democratic affairs: cotillions could be mistaken for army maneuvers carried out in long white dresses, especially as the camera captured such precision drills in the pages of *Life*. The Old Guard no longer had the spare cash for the extravaganzas of an earlier day; besides, high society seemed to have developed aristocratic inhibitions about flaunting one's wealth in wanton display. But the one-girl one-ball formula retained a certain fatal attraction, especially for those from cities without provision for the assemblies and clubs that managed debuts in Philadelphia, St. Louis, Baltimore, and elsewhere. A case in point was the "Party of the Century," the debutante ball thrown by Henry Ford II at the Detroit Country Club in 1959 for his daughter Charlotte.

Naturally, the $250,000 Ford debut loomed large in *Life:* the $60,000 worth of flowers; the massive renovation of the Grosse Pointe clubhouse, so it resembled an eighteenth-century French chateau. Numbered among the invitees were du Ponts, Roosevelts, Firestones, Churchills, and the Gary Coopers of Hollywood. Charlotte, looking plump and fairly ordinary in her strapless Dior gown (as opposed to the short, hot-pink Dior cocktail dress she had worn for the dinner earlier that evening), danced the first dance with her father and then jitterbugged away with an eighteen-member stag line of young swains, each of whom wore a medallion bearing Miss Ford's initials. The family received. Nat "King" Cole sang. Jacques Frank, the fashionable French decorator hired to oversee the transformation of the building, fussed with the imported magnolia leaves. New York hairdresser Julius Caruso, flown in for the day, repaired the deb's beehive from time to time. Bandleader

Meyer Davis uncorked a special song, entitled "Charlotte," which he had written for the occasion.

The last guest drifted away on a cloud of jazz—played in a smaller room done up as a bistro—at 7 A.M. "Bow's the Wow," indeed! The comings out of Barbara Hutton and Brenda Frazier paled by comparison. So did the few noteworthy individual debuts of the past decade: Betty Tyson's Newport dance, which cost a mere $40,000 and snared Douglas Fairbanks Jr. and a handful of Washington politicos as celebrity attendees. Another Widener ball, for Ella Anne, with Pershings, Biddles, and Vanderbilts on deck. The Nicole du Pont ball, held in tents designed by Valerian Rybar in a blinding combination of oranges and pinks.

Vogue may have covered those parties, but nothing equaled the Ford Ball of 1959. Unless it was the Anne Ford debut of 1961, also spotlighted in the pages of *Life*. This time, the party occupied a pavilion and two smaller summerhouses on the grounds of the Fords' Michigan estate. This time, Ella Fitzgerald sang. This time, Meyer Davis played a new number: "Man! That's Anne." The boys wore medallions again. Anne designed her own dress. Charlotte, a post-deb now, joined her in the receiving line. The imported hairdresser teased and sprayed. The party, said *Life*, "had stunned guests with its sumptuous splendor."

In the wake of Anne's bash, actress and comic writer Cornelia Otis Skinner hosted an hour-long TV show on debuting for NBC. Although the cameras were not allowed to penetrate the more venerable of the group cotillions, reviewers observed that individual balls were becoming few and far between. "It is true that the superlatively vulgar display of wealth that marked some of the deb balls in past years has been toned down in recent times," wrote a television critic. "But even today's deb parties are fabulous enough, and one cannot help wondering what place they have in a world becoming more and more conscious of the great gulfs that yawn between rich and poor." If all the money spent by the Fords on their recent debuts had been given directly to the needy, the gesture would not have solved the problem of poverty in America. But it might have given "the world a . . . more attractive image of the rich in the United States."

Instead, the world witnessed the Wanamaker debut of 1963 and its courtroom aftermath. The ball was held in Southampton, under a pink marquee on the lawn of the Leas estate. Mrs. Leas was the mother of seventeen-year-old Fernanda Wanamaker Wetherill of Philadelphia, great-great-granddaughter of John Wanamaker, the legendary retailer. In the beginning, everything seemed fine at Westerly. The deb wore white—and a big blonde beehive. There were the usual balloons and fountains and lighted torches, the champagne, the clutches of Fords and du Ponts, and the Duke of Marlborough mingling with the likes of cartoonist Charles Addams and movie star Joan Fontaine. But as a special feature of the night, Fernanda's stepfather had hired an eighteen-piece proto-rock band, El Corals, to play for the stags and the visiting debs after the "square" society orchestras had gone home. The afterparty went on until after dawn, when 150 young persons, all registered on the official list, moved themselves and the band down the beach to a forty-room vacant mansion Mr. Leas had rented to house the stags overnight. And then the assorted college boys and gate-crashers proceeded to trash the place. "It was like walking into a pigpen," said the local chief of police, called to the scene by neighbors. "It looked like a bomb hit." Windows smashed. Broken furniture strewn along the shoreline. Cans and bottles and glass everywhere. Boys with hangovers asleep where they fell. "Each thing seemed funnier than the last," remarked one of the vandals. "It was great."

Damage estimates varied wildly, from $3,000 for broken windows to $10,000 for mass destruction. Perpetrators and gawkers sold snapshots of the wreckage to Luce and to the tabloids. Fernanda Wetherill's ball was the society scandal of the decade. Why did they do it? asked a psychoanalyst hired by Henry Luce. "The boys," he decided, "were working off serious quantities of pent-up aggression and hostility." But what did rich boys like these have to be hostile about? Were they the victims of a mass psychosis fueled by permissiveness, too much money, and rock 'n' roll? In the spring of 1964, when the matter finally came to court, the seven ringleaders were released on payment of $6,000. One witness said he couldn't recall what happened because he had passed out. Another excused himself from any serious mayhem: "I was dancing on a table when someone body-checked me and I went through the French doors. That's all the damage I did." Fernanda was offered a four-year movie contract and a role in the next James Bond film. "I never really had any enthusiasm for deb parties," she told the flock of reporters gathered outside the Suffolk County Courthouse. "I really didn't get any pleasure out of them at all."

The beautiful, silly, rich-girl, dabbling deb became one of the sturdiest archetypes of the mid-twentieth century. With her pinky upraised and her makeup excessive, she was the glamorous figure on the cover of a "Debutantes" paper-doll book. Her patois inspired comic dictionaries of How to Talk Deb: "Bed," for instance, was defined in one such lexicon as "a sleeping couch occupied by a debutante from sunrise to midday, by a Working Girl from midnight to sunrise. (Not the same bed, of course.)" The lyrics of a Rogers and Hart song make fun of Brenda Frazier and her kind. "I'll make money and I'll make it quick," sings the debutante on the make. "Boosting cigarettes that make me sick!" Alfred Hitchcock's *The Lady Vanishes* (1938) stars a jaded, dithery, but oh-so-soigné English deb about to marry a boring blue blood until a murder aboard a train brings her to her senses.

In the first version of *The Philadelphia Story* (1940), the moviegoer needs no cotillion to identify Katharine Hepburn ("Miss Tracy Lord") as a Main Line deb being stalked on the eve of her wedding by a reporter from *Spy* magazine. Her dialogue is brittle, her paper-doll poses exaggerated, her wardrobe (by Adrian) expensive—and her behavior just as mannered when she is being herself as when the fictional Miss Lord is trying to throw the press off the scent. The 1956 remake, *High Society* starring Grace Kelly, is only loosely based on the original. Or rather, it seems to spring directly from the poor little rich girl stereotype of the 1930s, supplemented by the deb-like looks and persona of Miss Kelly, a wealthy girl from Philadelphia in real life. Alas, Grace's patrician demeanor and her ringside appearances at "21" had not made her eligible for invitations to the local cotillions: she was a Catholic, her parents were the children of first-generation immigrants, and despite the family's wealth, Main Line society simply did not admit her kind. In a sense, then, *High Society,* set among the rich of Newport in the early 1950s, was the debut Grace Kelly never got.

In a sense, too, the story is not really about the 1950s, but about the afterglow of Brenda Frazier's era, the last days of café society. Kelly's ex-husband, played by Bing Crosby, is a rich jazz baby: whenever he turns up in the course of the film, Louis Armstrong is sure to follow. Armstrong was "cool" personified, pepper to the salt of high society and a symbol of "advanced" taste in a decade of racial apartheid. And if the Henry Fords could summon Nat "King" Cole and Ella Fitzgerald for command performances, why, Miss Kelly had to have a black superstar too. Frank Sinatra, equally cool, plays the pesky society reporter in this version of the story, adding another dimension of laid-back sophistication to the rituals of the other half. He sings witty Cole Porter tunes. And he's got Grace's number: "publicity, they love it!" he exclaims when his Blue Book subjects feign horror at being photographed for the tabloids.

The upcoming society wedding, white dress and all, functions as part of an elaborate debut that begins with a ball at an old Newport estate. As the music plays and the dancers circle the room, Kelly gets roaringly, adorably drunk and finds herself bound for a midnight swim with the plebian Sinatra. Her antics are both a reflection of debdom past and a premonition of follies to come. She could be Fernanda. Or Brenda. Or Charlotte. Or Anne.

M rs. Burnham Hockaday had a splendid idea. Why not have a grand ball in Kansas City once a year? In the spring, when Missouri showed itself off to best advantage. In the gorgeous, becolumned Kirkwood Hall of the art museum, the most beautiful place in the city. What fun!

The Burnham Hockadays were one of oldest and "best" families in the state, with deep roots in the history of central Missouri. Although the Hockadays and their Rollins kin were not the richest residents of the district surrounding the museum and Country Club Plaza—Burnham was a manufacturer's agent—they nonetheless had great social clout. So when Clara Hockaday began dreaming of an annual ball, her friends took notice. In 1953, only six years after arriving in Kansas City, she was already president of the women's division of the local Philharmonic orchestra. The orchestra was deeply in debt. The museum was a focus of civic pride. Why not mount a *benefit* ball to raise the necessary funds, right there in the marble halls of the Nelson-Atkins Museum of Art?

DEBBING FOR A GOOD CAUSE

The more she talked about a formal ball, the greater the interest. A core group of fourteen prominent men and women called on one of the museum trustees, who took the matter under advisement for six months. Finally, as the Hockadays vacationed in Hot Springs, Arkansas, the word came down: the art gallery would play host to the ball. When Clara Hockaday returned to town, she entertained fifty movers and shakers at a cocktail party at her home to iron out details and involve a broader spectrum of Kansas City socialites. At the party, one guest suggested that the event be called the Jewel Ball—and that a piece of jewelry be presented to one of the guests as the high point of the evening.

It was also determined that Mrs. R. Crosby Kemper, the undisputed doyenne of local society, be named chairperson of the ball. And she, in turn, suggested that debutante presentations be part of the proceedings to engage the interest of the community more fully. Everybody had a daughter, a granddaughter, a favorite niece, she reasoned. Everybody liked to see pretty debs bowing and waltzing into society in their long gloves and their virginal white gowns.

And so the deed was done. Committees were formed. Businesses were approached for contributions in kind. Patrons were enlisted, whose ticket fees would cover operating expenses. A secret panel of matrons drew up a list of acceptable young women who met a number of criteria: the family must have made noteworthy contributions to civic life; they must have lived in the area for ten years or more; and the candidate herself must have completed her freshman year in college. Bids went out to the chosen few—twenty-six potential debutantes. In later years, when the Jewel Ball had become a permanent fixture on the Kansas City social calendar, the founders speculated that it was really a coming-of-age ritual for the city, still insecure about its reputation as a "cow town." Tiaras and long gloves were the means of changing that image.

But, as history records, the ball almost didn't happen. The gala evening was slated for June 2, 1954. Invitations were issued. Contracts were written. Only then did the organizers discover that college freshmen and their friends had final exams; they would not be home from school on June 2. The date was hastily moved to the twenty-fifth, rehearsals were cut to two brief run-throughs of the waltz (with music provided by a lone accordion), and Mesdames Kemper and Hockaday held their breath. There were glitches. Two debs from Smith turned up in identical gowns, bought off the rack from the only store near campus that stocked long dresses. Even mothers shopping for dresses on behalf of debs encountered problems. Because the ball came together so quickly, the Kansas City department stores had no chance to stock suitable attire. One girl borrowed the dress her older sister had worn when she came out in Little Rock in 1949. Looking back on the ball twenty-five years later, another deb said, "Mine was the ugliest dress I ever had in my life." Nobody realized that social history was being made that very hot night in 1954. Some of those on the original list opted to go to

Making a bow at the Jewel Ball in Kansas City, 1959. Western Historical Manuscript Collection—Kansas City

Europe for the summer and skip the ball. Others were puzzled by the fuss. "I really didn't quite understand what it was all about until it was almost over," admitted Mrs. Graham Hunt, the former Judith Henry, years afterward. "There was nothing to relate it to. The importance didn't come through initially, but it was extraordinarily different."

Despite a shaky start, the first Jewel Ball was a great success, a "fairyland," said the *Kansas City Star* the next morning, "a magic temple of glittering lights, a panorama of loveliness." At 10 P.M., to the strains of the march from *Aida*, twenty-three debutantes and their fathers entered the hall in solemn procession. Each girl came forward on her father's arm and made a deep curtsy to the crowd. When everybody had bowed, fathers and daughters danced a waltz to the strains of the "Blue Danube," the designated escorts cut in, and finally, the patrons, the relatives—anyone with the price of a tux and a $10 ticket—joined in the grand finale. A supper was served. And at midnight, a diamond necklace—the "Midnight Necklace," with seventy-seven stones totaling 9.92 carats—was solemnly borne into Kirkwood Hall on a pillow by a little girl dressed as a page. A ticket stub was drawn. The donated jewel of the first Jewel Ball was won by a lady who was not present at that late hour.

Of course there were zippers that failed to zip; pandemonium reigned in the gallery hastily turned into a dressing room for the night. Young men and their mothers worried that the white dinner jackets required of escorts, worn on the previous evening at a formal dance at the Mission Hills Country Club, would not come back from the cleaner's in time. Traffic backed up in the circular drive in front of the museum as curious motorists drove by to enjoy the spectacle. In the end however, the Jewel Ball was a triumph. The thirteen hundred guests had a fine time, and $10,000 went toward the Philharmonic's deficit. By March 1955, the committees were at it again. New pages had been recruited, a fifty-eight-carat blue topaz "jewel" donated by a consortium of four local jewelers, a preview of the ball was scheduled by a local TV station, and the museum was added to the list of beneficiaries. The names of the patrons were listed in the newspapers. So were those of the escorts—and the debs.

Stores were advertising dresses not for the debutantes but for the lady leaders of the various committees and subcommittees. One of the novel features of the mass debut was that what the matrons wore was of greater import than the deb "uniform" of white dress and accessories. Those in charge of decorations or food or publicity composed detailed descriptions of their attire for the press long before the big night arrived. For Mrs. Kemper's first term as chair of the ball, for instance, she "was gowned in a pink shantung dress embroidered with pink crystal beads. The skirt was voluminous and she wore matching pink shoes." The buds were praised for a "youthful glow" enhanced by their simple gowns. But their costumes were of little interest compared with those of the gaudy gems of the Jewel Ball in their aqua sheaths and emerald bouffants. By the 1960s, the eye-popping dresses of the grown-ups were being iden-

Debs do the traditional waltz with their fathers in Kirkwood Hall at the Nelson-Atkins Gallery in Kansas City. Western Historical Manuscript Collection—Kansas City

tified by name: Oscar de la Renta, Christian Dior, Helen Rose, Norman Norell.

Before World War II, the most celebrated debs came out at "private" balls at which only one girl was presented; their elders, even when unmarried, were not supposed to be the belles of the ball. Despite her awkwardness, Barbara Hutton's debut dance was hers alone. The private ball was a perfect means of concentrating the publicity barrage on a single young woman: on her special night, competition was not encouraged. And as an occasion for conspicuous (or contemptuous) consumption, the individual debut had no equal. Society editors turned rosters of titled guests and estimates of wild expenditure into front-page news.

Debs in waiting: the pages who bear the jewel at the Jewel Ball, 1961. Western Historical Manuscript Collection—Kansas City

As private fortunes fell victim to income taxes and corporate scrutiny, as postwar shortages made outrageous displays of lucre unseemly, and as young women joined returning GIs in the college classroom and in the ranks of white-collar workers, the all-out, end-of-the-world deb party for one little bud fell out of fashion. It did not disappear, to be sure: the Fords and the Wideners kept to the old ways, and the oil millionaires of Texas—the real-life models for the characters in Edna Ferber's *Giant*—indulged themselves in deb follies of Texan proportions. But the social pendulum in the nation as a whole swung in the direction of moderation. Buds began to bloom en masse, at coming-out events staged for worthy causes. Or for the sake of old and venerable traditions. Or for civic betterment. The Jewel Ball, which celebrated its forty-seventh anniversary in 2000, is one of the leading products of this 1940s and 1950s shift to debbing for charity.

Changes came slowly over the years. The deb procession was routed one way and then another. One bow became three or four curtsies at various points in the museum, so that each girl could be seen by each and every guest. One year, a car was raffled off, in addition to the jewel. The badges—satin rosettes identifying patrons and junior patrons—changed color and shape. Bandleaders came and went: Lester Lanin and Meyer Davis were hired several times because they also played at high-profile New York balls, but they were expensive. Bands from St. Louis were cheaper. So was Al Madison, who worked the prom and country-club circuit on the East Coast at bargain rates because the members of his smallish band all played several instruments. In 1965, he wrote the singable, danceable "Jewel Waltz" especially for Kansas City.

But Mrs. Hockaday, the perennial head of the committee in charge of the music, and Enid Kemper, a fixture at the post of honorary chair, had higher aspirations for the ball than merely increasing annual revenues and providing a splendid night's entertainment. The Jewel Ball, said Mrs. Kemper in 1960, "is a means of teaching the debutantes their role in assuming responsibilities in the community." Post-debs were expected to take their places on Jewel Ball committees. Mandatory tours of the museum made new debutantes aware of the city's treasures and their duty to preserve them.

In 1983, *Kansas City* magazine took a long look back at the Jewel Ball debs of 1963 to see what the eighteen girls who had come out during the presidency of John F. Kennedy had done with their lives. In 1963, the general public still enjoyed reading about debutantes and their parties: the beautiful and cultured Mrs. Kennedy had been a famous deb in her time. But what had happened to the Kansas City debs who had lived on, through the women's movement and Vietnam? A third of them became housewives; some of the husbands were escorts from the ball. One

Twelve young socialites, looking very much like queens in their elegant white gowns, made their formal bows to Houston Society on Saturday, November 9 in the Regency Room of the Shamrock Hilton Hotel.

For the charming debutantes, it was a regal moment . . . a lyric and enchanting prelude signaturing their debut to an exquisite symphony of social activity, a season embellished with joy and happiness.

As is our yearly custom, we dedicate this December issue of Houston Town & Country to the debutantes, their proud families and friends, and the members of Allegro. The picture above, and those of the debutantes with their escorts, were all taken by Gittings of Houston on the evening of the Allegro Ball presentation.

Allegro

Miss Jessie Taylor Otto, daughter of Mr. and Mrs. Bruce A. Wilson, 10007 Briar Drive. Miss Otto was presented at Allegro by her father.

November 9, 1968

A page from the 1968 debutante scrapbook of Miss Jessie Taylor Otto of Houston, Texas.
Jessie Otto Hite

debutante was a soap-opera star, another a businesswoman, a third a psychologist and consultant. A divorcée confessed to having enjoyed the ball at the time, even though she had participated because it was important to her parents. After college and a failed marriage, however, she found herself in charge of a thriving enterprise in Ohio, having learned that "the individual was much more important, not who their parents were." But the majority were active in civic affairs, wherever they landed, and remembered the Jewel Ball with real fondness.

It was "an unreal, fun world," said a woman who had left Kansas City behind almost as soon as the music stopped playing. "For ten days you're at a series of parties and nothing is serious. It's also the last summer I was home. I remember it as kind of the last free summer." A magazine editor in New York credited the Jewel Ball with giving her the "kind of social grace . . . that sets you apart." She loved "the lights, the gowns, the flowers [fifteen hundred pink carnations in 1963]. It was just a whirl of extravagance. It was so much bigger than any of us." The son of one of the 1963 debs was an escort at the 1983 ball. None of the women polled regretted her debut. It was a grand highlight in a series of interesting, useful lives.

KEEPING IT EXCLUSIVE: SOCIETY MEETS REALITY

To date, three crises have momentarily dimmed the sparkle of the Jewel Ball. The first involved religious prejudice; the second, class; and the third, race. A handwritten report on the deliberations of the "secret" committee that selected the debutantes for 1960 contains, after the list of the chosen twenty-five, a single name, #26, scrawled at the bottom of the page by someone other than the chair of the group. The report continues: "We wish to call to the attention of the steering committee that we think you should consider carefully the problem that will occur by the exclusion" of #26 "because of her family's great and continued financial support of the Philharmonic." In fact, the grandfather of the deb in question had been a leading Kansas City entrepreneur and philanthropist who not only supported the orchestra but also promoted the love of music by giving free tickets to his customers and paying the Philharmonic to play along with pop entertainers in special concerts for anyone who cared to attend.

He was Jewish, however, and Kansas City society was rigidly structured along "separate but equal" lines to keep Jews out. There was, for example, a Jewish country club, and anti-Semitic social leaders interviewed about this obvious schism always claimed that everyone was more comfortable in his or her own "set." Although at least one prominent Jewish family was deeply involved in both the Jewel Ball and the affairs of the museum in the 1960s, there seems to have been a tacit agreement that Jewishness was not to be an issue in their case, and their case alone. In the end, Miss 26 joined the ranks of the 1960 debutantes. Her mother, resplendent in "geranium pink organza with panniers from shoulders to the floor," beamed as her daughter bowed to the gentile elite. Eventually, the daughters and nieces and cousins of the controversial deb would take their places in Kirkwood Hall, too.

But there was no general loosening of the tacit exclusion of all but white Anglo-Saxon Protestants (and a spattering of Catholics) from the ranks of social acceptability. Since the reason for drawing up lists and publishing *Social Registers* in the first place is to separate "us" from "them," it is not surprising that prejudice should be a major factor in the selection of debutantes. What is surprising is the recognition that, under the published rules, #26 deserved to take her place in Kansas City's Jewel Ball.

Ten years later, another incident disrupted the stately progress of the seventeenth grand promenade. An anonymous tipster told a museum guard that a time bomb had been planted in the building and was set to explode at 12:20 A.M., just as the jewel was being awarded, or so the papers said. In the meantime, an unruly crowd of "hippies" had gathered in a nearby park, shouting obscenities and threatening to charge across the south lawn straight into Kirkwood Hall. Police were called to the scene. Tear gas was used to disperse the mob, and order was restored by the time the festivities began to wind down. Only the smell of tear gas remained as a memorial to the Battle of the Jewel Ball.

In the clear light of day, however, the skirmish was soon reduced to a farce. Two young men—an army veteran and a college kid home for the summer—had been hanging out in the park when they noticed the bright lights in the museum and went to take a look. They were met by officers with snarling dogs and told that the grounds were off-limits, by order of the chief of police. This angered the group in the park. Cans

When is a deb not a deb? Jewish girls did not customarily "come out" in Minnesota in 1963, but an indulgent aunt had James Rea paint her niece in deb regalia anyway. Minnesota Historical Society

and bottles flew. Tear gas was fired. Everyone went home, except for the two young men who had wanted a look at the debutantes. They bought fifteen cups of coffee, came back to the park, and handed them out to the police who stood guard over the Jewel Ball as if awaiting an invading army.

Was it an out-of-control "demonstration" against the ball, as the law believed, or just another hot night in Kansas City? The police presence suggests a certain unease on the part of the museum and the Jewel Ball hierarchy—a fear of mobs, of disapproval on the part of oddly dressed persons omitted from the guest list: the envious non-elite. Even in 1970, the Jewel Ball was an anachronism. "In a time when so much is going on and changing, it's one of the few things in this world that hasn't changed," said the mother of a local debutante. But perhaps change was in order. In the early 1980s, a congresswoman who had attended many debut balls in the 1950s was asked her opinion on the Jewel Ball and its counterparts elsewhere. Parties for the young are fine, she opined. But "when times are hard, when people are poor and suffering, you ought to think pretty hard before you have a frightfully extravagant display of wealth." Or when you threaten to arrest other youngsters for wanting to catch a glimpse of your party, or to walk on the lawn of the city's landmark art museum.

In the spring of 1991, the exclusionary policies of the ruling caste collided with the facts of a multiracial, multicultural America. The question of the hour? Had the ladies of the Jewel Ball deliberately omitted the newly elected mayor from the guest list because he was black? The socialites said no: the invitation was in the mail. Lost. Misplaced. The chairwoman hand-delivered a replacement to City Hall within hours of the complaint. Would Emanuel Cleaver and his wife, Dianne, come? The Cleavers deliberated while the Kansas City press had a field day with the recent embarrassments of the rich and powerful. The Jewel Ball, it was noted, had never chosen a black debutante. Mayors, however, had always been invited. Recently, the Kansas City Country Club's admissions policies had made national headlines when pro golfer Tom Watson resigned to protest the de facto ban on racial and religious minorities. Was this another bad mark against the city? What would the mayor do? More to the point, what would the Jewel Ball committee do?

On the night of the thirty-eighth ball, the Cleavers—and the cameras—arrived at the doors of the gallery a scant eight minutes after they opened, to handshakes and cordiality all around. The mayor wore white tie, his wife a black sequined sheath with a plunging backline. Before the couple ducked inside, Cleaver told reporters that their presence was symbolic of "the inclusiveness all of us in Kansas City would really like to see." They left at eleven o'clock for another function. Had he enjoyed himself? the mayor was asked. He had, he said, "as much fun as you can have at a debutante ball." Mayor Cleaver came back the following year, with almost as much fanfare. "This is no different than what we've been struggling for for four thousand years, but it feels a lot more comfortable than it did twelve months ago," said the first African-American ever to witness the Jewel Ball. This time, he was joined by the president of the local chapter of the NAACP, a longtime supporter of the museum and what was now called the Kansas City Symphony. "Tradition is very difficult to transcend," they allowed, but perhaps progress was being made at last.

Laura Rollins Hockaday, Clara's daughter, had become society editor of the *Star* and took pains to keep the debate over diversity and debuts alive throughout the 1990s. It was she who pointed out that tradition—not exclusion—was the most crucial element in the success of the Jewel Ball. It was a matter of families, continuity, the cultural underpinnings of the city. The older Alpha Kappa Alpha Debutante Ball, Laura Hockaday observed, had never invited a white debutante. The Noche de Gala, put on by the Hispanic community, honored its first male participant in 1993. And there were other balls, other debut events, for high school seniors, for disadvantaged youth, for ethnic groups, and even for the segment of Kansas City society involved in the annual American Royal Show—of livestock. Coming out had never been more democratic.

The self-presentation of the Jewel Ball also changed markedly: the women who chaired the event in the 1950s had done so simply on the basis of their social standing, or so the papers implied. But lengthy stories about the lives of the principals began to appear in the local press in the 1960s. These articles were full-blown biographies describing the women's education, family histories, and involvement in civic affairs. If the debs of Kansas City—and their doting moms—did not burn their bras in Kirkwood Hall, they did assert their importance to their community as women and, more important, as individuals.

Richard Nixon's daughter Julie, who made her formal debut before her father took up residence in the White House, signed notes to family members "N.C.P.D.," or "no cream-puff deb." The term applies nicely to Enid Kemper, Clara Hockaday, and their successors. Although women had entered the arena of public affairs in the nineteenth century primarily through their management of social spectacles, the women's movement of the 1960s and 1970s was not just about career equity. Wives and mothers active in Kansas City society asserted their right to recognition on the basis of their organizational abilities, volunteerism, and interest in civic betterment campaigns. The same women who promoted the Jewel Ball also worked for civil rights, antipoverty campaigns, literacy programs, and a variety of schemes to raise money for local cultural institutions. They were not cream-puff debs but women to be reckoned with.

DEBS OR QUEENS?

And the Jewel Ball, as Laura Hockaday asserted, was hardly the only game in town. Beginning in the late 1940s, the American Royal Livestock and Horse Show began to edge its way into the debutante business. The annual American Royal Show was a major midwestern event. Thousands of participants swelled the coffers of Kansas City merchants and hotel keepers. The show was also a point of great civic pride: it made Kansas City the nation's center of the trade in blooded stock. Kansas City bankers, shippers, and suppliers, along with the service industries, exerted themselves mightily on behalf of the show and took active roles in its governing association. So it was that Kempers and Hockadays and Nicolses helped shape the social events surrounding the fall exposition. While New York debs displayed themselves at the annual Horse Show, Kansas City debs shared the spotlight with the aristocrats of the animal kingdom.

In 1947, the American Royal announced that it would hold an annual "queen" contest at the time of the show. Fifty closely chaperoned young women—the first batch of candidates—were chosen from families active in horse and cattle breeding in a five-state area and were given special pins to mark the honor. The winner was promised a fifty-piece wardrobe contributed by the Kansas City Apparel Association and a white designer gown for the coronation. In past years, compacts or other tokens had been given to candidates. But with the special pin, it was hoped that a sorority of queens and also-rans could be established, girls who would help the organizers in future years. The title of American Royal Queen was highly coveted. Small communities across the corn belt held local pageants to select their contestants, and in 1953, President Eisenhower, a Kansas boy himself, was expected to attend the festivities.

The announcer that year was Sarah Churchill, daughter of Britain's doughty Prime Minister and frequent hostess on the Hallmark Hall of Fame television show (sponsored by the Halls of Kansas City). The elaborate program consisted of a dance number by the Royalettes, fifty high school girls; a skit by TV cowboys, "The Cisco Kid and Pancho"; a procession of the Belles of the American Royal and their escorts, who performed a waltz; and the coronation of the lucky girl, with a raft of television personalities presiding. The Friday night Coronation Ball heralded the official start of the American Royal Show. On Saturday morning, Her Majesty proceeded through downtown on a float, and the judging of animals raised by members of the Future Farmers of America (FFA) began, with the new queen in attendance.

The Coronation Ball, with its cast of national celebrities, was a harvest festival of sorts, a larger version of the state fairs at which celebration of a successful crop went hand in hand with entertainment and a variety of contests in which the "best" in a particular category of items was selected: blue-ribbon jam, quilts, sheep, infants—or beauty queens. The emphasis on the superior breeding of plants and animals spilled over into human eugenics on these occasions. FFA and 4-H members learned how to breed better calves. "Healthy Boy and Girl" and "Better Baby" contests regularly held at state fairs in Minnesota, Iowa, and Kansas encouraged farmers and spectators alike to see beautiful young women in similar terms, as potential mothers of superior stock. Although debutante balls had always carried with them the notion that a deb was now sexually mature and available for marriage, the queen contests in farm states made the purpose of processions and quadrilles and special costuming readily apparent.

In the mid-1950s, discussions of the Coronation Ball began to include frequent mention of the BOTARS (Belles of the American Royal Show), "official hostesses to the queen and the American Royal" organization, described as "outstanding young women of Kansas City" who ministered to the needs of aspiring queens. Gradually, the queen's importance dwindled, the ball moved into less agrarian quarters, and the BOTARS became the focus of Coronation Weekend. In 1960, the thirteenth class of BOTARS was selected by a secret committee on the basis of beauty, poise, "family background and contribution to civic activities." In private, American Royal officials called the group the "BOTARS and matrimonial society." Like the debutantes at the museum, they rehearsed long hours for their special number, a Viennese waltz at the beginning of the evening. Like the debs, they were entertained at luncheons and teas, and often in the same clubs and stately homes. The 1960 BOTARS sisterhood included Laura Hockaday and Nancy Nichols, the latter a member of the family that had built Country Club Plaza and developed the posh residential district around it. The BOTARS learned that they had been chosen when a special parchment scroll reached them early in August: the arrival of the herald persuaded several to change their plans for the fall, so great was the honor.

The Coronation Ball was steeped in tradition, albeit some of the customs were of recent origin. The BOTARS, for example, always wore identical gowns chosen by committee members at a special showing. They carried huge feathered fans, too, as they waltzed before the various princesses seated at one end of the hall. By 1965, there were more than three hundred alumnae of the BOTARS organization, including names already familiar to regular readers of the society columns. Past and present BOTARS began to raise money for their own group's affairs; in 1966, for example, they held a combined livestock auction and rock-and-roll dance to support the cost of feathers and dresses.

If the belles were not debs, they behaved as though they were. In the 1970s, their fathers escorted them into the hall for formal presentations, and the queens disappeared after twenty-eight years worth of Coronation Balls. Long lists of BOTARS and their genealogies replaced excited discussions of rural princessess; the city girls—past school age, for the most part—came from "prominent families" with impeccable pedigrees. They still wore matching dresses, but the dresses were often white and girlish now. In 1970, they were entertained at a formal tea by Mrs. Kemper, whose husband was vice-president of the Royal Association.

Many credit Harry Darby, Kansas City industrialist and former senator, with involving high society in a regional horse fair. Darby was the founder of the BOTARS and was instrumental in coaxing the black-tie crowd to the fund-raising ball in such droves that the beginning of the Kansas City social season was said to fall on that evening, when the girls bowed to the crowd and began to waltz. Meanwhile, the queen was chosen by others, and the BOTARS, in gowns of blue or black-and-white or glittering gold, danced to the music of society orchestras in the fancy ballrooms of Kansas City's new Crown Center hotels. It was an expensive honor. Fathers paid $500 to the American Royal organization to accept the invitation for their daughters to join the BOTARS. Parents were expected to host their share of parties, with bands and food and open bars. The clothes added to the big tab.

COTILLIONS AND CIVIC BETTERMENT

Some BOTARS complained that it was all too upper middle class. While the young women envisioned a tilt away from white-bread Protestantism, the American Royal thought that it had done its duty, the debs said, by inviting two girls who lived north of the Missouri River and a few with Irish-sounding surnames. And they complained vociferously when a news story said that they all wanted to marry their escorts. Most recent BOTARS are out of college and well launched on careers, they insist to the present day. No cream-puff debs at the American Royal Ball!

In the 1950s and 1960s, as Kansas City reveled in lists, white gowns, and the semi-secret rites of debdom, its social leaders sought to legitimate their newly minted traditions by putting the Jewel Ball and the various BOTAR events into both national and historical contexts. In 1958, the *Kansas City Star* revealed that the matriarchy of the Jewel Ball had used for its blueprint a similar, unnamed Chicago gala, limited to thirty young ladies. In fact, the correspondence of the 1959 chairwoman identifies the prototype as the Passavant Hospital Fund Ball in Chicago. "Really," she wrote, "the committee pretty much worked out the details . . . to fit Kansas City."

By 1959, however, the Jewel Ball itself had become the model for smaller cities that aspired to fund worthy causes with the fees collected from debs' doting fathers. The Albany, New York, Institute of History and Art and the "Bal du Lac" staged for the benefit of the Milwaukee Art Center were among several groups seeking advice, encouragement, and the creation of an informal network of outside–of–New York debutante venues. The *Boston Herald* ran a glowing account of the Jewel Ball in 1958, pointing out that more than $30,000 had been raised for the arts in a single season. "Yes," noted the article, "there ARE debutante parties west of Dedham." The sudden fame of the Jewel Ball was not entirely fortuitous. Successive committee members and well-connected friends of committee members wrote to *Life, Vogue,* and *Town and Country* seeking national coverage. Inducements were offered: debs could be photographed alongside art masterpieces in the museum's galleries, and the ladies in charge promised to fly their couturier gowns in from Paris for a pre-ball fashion show.

By the late 1950s, Kansas City debs were on the guest list of the Versailles Debutante Ball, where they expected to mingle with the cream of Europe's aristocrats, and were earnestly solicited to add their names to a national *Debutante Register* that already included "the North Carolina Terpsichorean, all of the New York balls, the Delta Debutante Ball, the Debutante Club of Mississippi, the Ak-Sar-Ben of Nebraska, the Orlando Country Club, the Clearwater Debut Ball of Florida, the Presentation Ball of Chicago, the Coronet Debutante Ball of Beverly Hills, and the Denver Symphony Debut Ball." The wildly varied listing of balls points to the renewed postwar popularity of debbing, especially when the ritual was linked to a worthy and impeccably genteel cause.

But group debuts like the Jewel Ball also evoked historical precedents, linking newly minted rituals with the stately manners of the past. An amateur historian working for the Jewel Ball compiled an impressive ancestry for the Kansas City debut-benefit, going back to the Philadelphia Dancing Assembly, founded in 1748, and venerable presentations in colonial Richmond and Charleston. If charity had not been the original object of these ancient cotillions, then there was the more modern Cinderella Ball of Fort Worth, Texas, the proceeds from which went to the local children's hospital. The jeweled coach of Cinderella, the chief decorative motif of the ball, was certainly in keeping with the theme in Kansas City.

The aim of these forays into history was clear: to legitimate a new social institution in a midwestern "cow town" by its affinity with the benevolence and mannerly graces of other places at other times. Kansas City aspired to become a new Philadelphia or, failing that, a new Fort Worth, bumptious, perhaps, but charitable and bighearted. At the same time, however, a second homegrown genesis for Kansas City debbing— much less distinguished—was also being rediscovered. This was the Priests of Pallas festival, held in the autumn from the 1880s until 1924. Centered on a grand parade, the Priests of Pallas gala was distantly related to Mardi Gras in its use of arcane mumbo-jumbo and an aura of mystery to draw tourists from the hinterland to the city and its merchants, hotels, and sundry attractions. Like Sinclair Lewis's Babbitt, a businessman who "boosted" his hometown at every opportunity, the Priests tailored their festival to assert the hegemony of Kansas City in the agricultural heartland. The parade, at first, featured beautiful women driving carriages bedecked with flowers. Later, the ladies and the flowers rode floats mounted on trolley cars, making this "the first electrical parade ever given in the U.S.A." But the climax of the week came with the elegant formal ball, at which spectators stood for hours to catch a glimpse of the queen ("Pallas Athene") and her maids of honor. Who would she be? What would she wear?

In 1924, the queen was Miss Edna Marie Peck, a recent debutante, who mounted to her throne in the Convention Center in a silver sheath with panniers of electric blue tulle. She wore a crown of rhinestones and carried a huge fan. Surrounding the queen were the members of her court, chosen by the young men's division of the Priests. The affair was written up in detail in the next morning's papers and quoted in 1960, when a 1924 maid of honor became the new head of the Jewel Ball: "Following the dictates of fashion, a number of these beauties were presented on future dates to Kansas City Society at elaborate debut parties given by their parents. Others 'made their bow' at lavish entertainments given in groups, from which evolved the Jewel Ball." The debutante and her sisters stood for the democracy of the group "bow," the distinction of old families, the benevolence of charitable giving, the importance of the city, the heritage of the nation, and the precious beauty of youth. And more, much more. Parental pride. Hope for the future. The deb was the jewel in the crown of the heartland. A lover of culture. A cosmopolitan in the making. A star.

In 1978, a special issue of the Sunday magazine published by the *Kansas City Star* weighed and measured her once more against all those other debutantes. Kansas City, the authors concluded, was home to "the largest concentration of privilege between St. Louis and San Francisco (not counting Texas, which everybody knows is tacky)." So it was a natural hotbed of debbing. Yet Kansas City debs weren't snooty, like the pseudo-aristocracy of Boston and Charleston. They worked hard on matters of civic betterment. They were mostly white and Protestant. And well-off. Elsewhere, the tide was turning against secret lists and selection committees. New group debuts had loosened up the exclusivity of the social ranks. Throughout the 1960s and 1970s, closed circles were being pried open or sidestepped altogether.

In Atlanta—where debs' silver patterns were listed in the *Constitution*—a Phoenix Society was established to introduce girls who were not members of the old Debutante Club. In Chicago, where WASP society came out at the Passavant Ball, the Catholics (Presentation Ball), Jews (Ambassadors Ball), African-Americans (Links Ball), and Polish-Americans (White and Red Ball) all staged their own coming-out parties. And, as Cornelia Guest put it in 1986, "even the farm teams have their own debutante balls." A ball in Danville, Illinois, was patterned after the Passavant Cotillion. So were new balls from Southern California to Georgia, all citing mystic orders, time-honored cotillions, and charity as the reasons for the dresses and other paraphernalia of debitude.

A recent social history of Montgomery, Alabama, traces local balls back to the 1820s and Lafayette's ceremonial visit to the city. By 1841, an assembly was being held regularly by the True Blues and Dexter Fire Company No. 1, and the first debutante presentation took place in 1862, when a Confederate general brought out his daughter in the midst of the Civil War. A masked men's society, the Mystic Order of Revelry, inaugurated its New Year's Eve deb presentations in 1928. And so it went, with assemblies and cotillions, both black and white, revived in the 1960s and 1970s. "Those who do not understand how pleasant is an occasional suspension of reality have criticized the mystic and debutante balls for foolish extravagance," writes the appreciative husband of a former deb, who cherishes the beautiful gowns, the pseudo-suspense, the music, and the make-believe as particularly Southern ornaments of society.

But, as it had been in the days of the glamor deb, New York remained the apogee of debbing and the stronghold, some would argue, of the charity debutante ball. To New Yorkers, *the* cotillion is the Debutante Cotillion and Christmas Ball held for the benefit of the New York Infirmary. Inaugurated in 1935, when the Great Depression began to cast its shadow over individual debuts, the ball introduces about a hundred young women annually, with cotillion figures, beaming fathers, and long, white kid gloves. The Gotham Ball is virtually the same event, except that Catholic debs are presented to the reigning prelate. The Debutante Assembly and New Year's Ball, founded in 1931, and the Junior League Ball, founded in 1948, are other mass presentations of note in New York.

These and a host of lesser balls make up the city's busy debutante season, the topic of Whit Stillman's 1990 film *Metropolitan*, in which a group of preppies, home for the holidays from various Ivy League schools, attends all but identical deb balls every night and gathers afterward, in a jumble of half-empty cocktail glasses and souvenir beanies supplied by society orchestras, to speak of literature, philosophy, and the impending extinction of their class. The end-of-the-world ennui of *Metropolitan* makes a neat counterpoint to *The Mayflower Madame* of 1987, a movie based on the real-life exploits of Sidney Biddle Barrows, who came out in the Grand Ballroom of the Plaza at the annual deb ball sponsored by the Mayflower Society. Because her fame was predicated on the contrast between Ms. Barrows's later career as a high-priced madam and the demure deb in white peau de soie (from the Adam Room at Saks), the details of her debut provided ammunition to those who hoped to see the end of snobbery in the name of costly charity.

Her grandmother had been a "wildly popular debutante," wrote Sidney Barrows. She had grown up looking at the scrapbooks and the invitations of that earlier time. When her grandparents proposed that she come out in New York City, along with other descendants of the *Mayflower* Pilgrims, she was delighted. "The whole night was like a dream," she remembered, "and I kept hoping it would never end. . . . I felt like part of a movie set." As subsequent events would demonstrate, the starry-eyed young Sidney was the perfect Hollywood deb: a society beauty headed for a tragic fall—the heroine of a melodrama that came with its own props, sets, and costumes. A dream. A movie. A glorious pageant of beauty, class, and tinsel-topped splendor.

T here are almost as many kinds of debuts as there are cities. What suits Baltimore or Gotham may not play well west of the Mississippi. The in-house historians of Kansas City's Jewel Ball isolated several distinct strains of influence that shaped their own debutante presentation. One was the just-for-our-girl debut—the tea which became a reception and then a costly private dance—scaled back in the 1930s and 1940s to a group debut at a charity ball. Another was the dancing assembly, a colonial institution established for the purpose of promoting sociability in the crude new cities putting down roots along the East Coast. The Philadelphia assemblies of the eighteenth century, for example, were subscription dances arranged among like-minded friends. Membership fees paid for music, card rooms, and refreshments, and to ensure proper decorum, codes of conduct were adopted, "strict regulations as to the manner of conducting the dances." The rules mandated the hours of operation, the number of couples necessary to form a set for figure dancing, the authority of the director, and the obligation of the gentlemen-subscribers to distribute admission tickets only to suitable ladies.

THE DEBUT: AN AMERICAN INSTITUTION

Assemblies in Philadelphia, Charleston, Savannah, and elsewhere soon became gatekeeping mechanisms whereby the leading gentlemen of a given community controlled which young women, which families, and which potential husbands could enter their social circle. The white-tie Philadelphia Charity Ball, held for the 123rd time in December 2002, claims direct descent from the old subscription dances. The list of debutantes is short (about twenty in an average year), and the printed program is an elaborate document with full-color portraits of each deb posing alongside her parents and escort, in full regalia. The Bachelors Cotillon in Baltimore, formed in 1797, has a similar history: of its five annual germans, or balls, two have always been reserved for debutantes, chosen and escorted by members of the club. The first german, held in December, was tacitly acknowledged to include the "top" debs of the season. The second introduced the lesser lights. And the society columns of the *Baltimore Sun* were careful to record which young ladies were invited to the first Bachelors Cotillon and which to the second.

The St. Cecilia Society of Charleston traces its beginnings back to 1737 and an amateur music group; it became an assembly in 1819 in order to stage a ball in honor of President James Monroe's visit to the Carolinas. Here, too, the balls were run by men, who chose the debs until the late 1950s, when their stranglehold on Charleston social congress was eased slightly by a new debutante subcommittee composed of mothers of eligible girls. Nonetheless, most coming-out events based on the old male-dominated assemblies are still extremely selective and secretive, like the "krewes," or men's social clubs, of New Orleans, which pick the queens and courts for Mardi Gras balls from among the city's prettiest and best-bred debutantes.

To the outsider, Mardi Gras is a boozy series of parades and a few strings of souvenir beads tossed into the crowd of onlookers from floats bearing masked revelers aglitter with sequins. To the insider, it is a venerable ritual steeped in racial tension, secrecy, and a desire for social control. Paradoxically, Mardi Gras is also a classic carnival enacted at fever pitch: transgressive and boisterous. Some modern-day participants trace the idea of a pre-Lenten blowout to 1705, when masked figures ran riot in a French settlement near Mobile to celebrate their survival after a yellow fever epidemic. By 1722, when the capital of the French colony moved to New Orleans, so did the idea of Carnival, with its traditions of feasting, revelry, and license. Masked balls allowed for staged erotic encounters between white males and women of mixed blood (and vice versa). The first documented notice of Quadroon balls—for white men and free black women—came in 1805. The secrecy of such forbidden adventures was expressed in the obscure mythologies adopted by the krewes, of which the most famous in the nineteenth century were those of Comus, Momus, and Proteus. The public aspect of their activity consisted of masked processions or parades of Carnival royalty derived from the Grand March customary at balls. But the balls themselves were strictly private. Tickets were closely guarded; dance cards were works of art made of die-cut paper that unfolded into miniature tableaux and, since they came from the "gods" themselves, were delivered to the ladies by special courier.

By 1893, Proteus had instituted a system of "call-outs" for the first, most prestigious quadrilles at a given ball. The women to be featured in these dances were seated in a special section of the hall. Krewe members silently handed cards to the leaders bearing the names of the favored ladies, who were then "called out" publicly and escorted to their silent, heavily disguised partners. At the end of each quadrille, the female halves of the couples received favors that would often be handed down from generation to generation as a mark of a family's standing. Every ball also had a queen, and every queen had a court of fair maidens. Comus, in 1890, was last of the old-time krewes to adopt the custom.

Already, in the 1870s, the queens and their attendants were official debutantes, previously feted at teas and balls of their own, "American style." Indeed, white and Creole patriarchs remained active in krewes because they always had a fresh crop of daughters or granddaughters who needed a Carnival venue for the ultimate in coming-out parties. The queens were pictured in the society pages. They became local celebrities, remembered long after their reigns had ended. The biographies of debs always listed the royal pedigrees of their ancestors, who had been queens of Momus or maids of Proteus.

Henri Schindler, in his history of Mardi Gras, speculates that America's fascination with wealth, privilege, and royalty in the late nineteenth century created the milieu in which this extravagant style of debbing could flourish. Carnival queens of the 1890s appeared in national publications wearing gowns, trains, and crowns that would have been the envy of any reigning monarch. Paper favors were replaced by precious jewels. If they're lucky, the spectators who line the parade route today crying, "Hey, Mister! Throw me something, Mister!" get a string of purple plastic beads. These are dim reminders of the days when gold necklaces showered down on the throng from the hands of some benevolent figure, a rich man in disguise, the real ruler of New Orleans.

The Priests of Pallas masked balls held in Kansas City in the late nineteenth and early twentieth centuries were based in large part on Mardi

Gras. Kansas City businessmen customarily held an annual fall fair to bolster regional commerce. In 1887, President Grover Cleveland was slated to attend the festivities, and more than twenty thousand visitors came especially to see him. When Cleveland failed to appear, however, the crowd walked through the fairgrounds—and went home. Much to the chagrin of the organizers, "they were not in Kansas City fifteen minutes," lamented a local paper. A committee was formed immediately, of course, to figure out what would keep the day-trippers in Kansas City. It was their somewhat baffling conclusion that what people really craved was mystery. And so a delegation was sent to two cities that specialized in the mystical, the mythological, and the mysterious. New Orleans, with its Mardi Gras, was one of them—a tourist magnet even in the 1880s.

Soon after the committee's New Orleans expedition, a Kansas City krewe was formed, a ball and a parade organized, souvenirs ordered, and tickets delivered. The new secret club called itself the Priests of Pallas, in the belief that the name was so odd that it "would create talk and lend itself to advertisement." In the 1880s in western Missouri, it was still unthinkable that a respectable woman would ride a parade float, exposing herself to the public eye in so shameless a manner. So what women were required by the themes of the floats ("Mother Goose" in 1898 and "Grecian mythology" in 1887 and 1888, for example) were impersonated by Priests in wigs and skirts. Often, these pseudo-ladies were assailed by pranksters and hoodlums armed with peashooters. In the Show-Me State, the subjects on the sidewalk thus expressed a healthy contempt for any self-appointed ruling class of businessmen in regal disguise.

DAUGHTERS AS POLITICAL SYMBOLS

The second site that the future Priests of Pallas inspected in their quest for the most effective mixture of mumbo-jumbo and pageantry was St. Louis. St. Louis was the home of the Mystic Order of the Veiled Prophet, a secret society founded in 1878. Cornelia Otis Skinner later dubbed the Veiled Prophet (VP) Ball, the centerpiece of their annual rites, "the Ben-Hur of the debutante parties." At the time she made her quip, in the 1950s, festivities included a nighttime parade and a gala ball so spectacular that it merited a three-hour TV special. And the ball cul-

The Veiled Prophet himself, looking oh so mysterious, 1935. Missouri Historical Society

minated in the selection of a Queen of Love and Beauty and her maids of honor, perhaps the best publicized and most elaborately costumed debs in the nation. A local writer of the 1960s, after studying the history of the Prophets, decided that the costly, complicated rituals surrounding the annual debutante coronation indicated the survival of a neo-medieval "virgin cult" in the heartland.

One of the oddities of the Veiled Prophet phenomenon is how carefully it has been studied. Whereas making a debut has received almost no scholarly attention, and long-established community festivities little more, the Veiled Prophets have been the subject of two groundbreaking analyses. The first was a paper written for the Department of Anthropology at Harvard in 1947 by Allen Y. Davis, as part of his graduation requirements. The young Davis was convinced that "the ritual crowning of one of the year's debutantes as 'Queen of Love and Beauty'" was more than mere entertainment. On the contrary, he wrote, a pageant that engaged the energies of the city to such a degree must be "fulfilling certain needs in the community," which he set out to isolate. It was, Davis concluded, a "Rite of Intensification," defining St. Louis society along strictly stratified lines and conferring great prestige on the families of the chosen debutantes. In support of his argument, Davis further noted the gradual elimination of the parade and even of the ball, until only the coronation of a debutante remained as the focus for Veiled Prophet activity in the 1940s.

More recently, in a 2000 book on the history of the celebration, Thomas M. Spencer concentrates on political and economic power, contending that the earliest VP parade in 1878 came in the wake of a successful general strike. The masked figures parading through the streets of St. Louis were taking back the city in the name of a powerful but anonymous elite, asserting its control over the unruly masses. Early illustrations of the event show Prophets (incorrectly) in disguises not unlike those of the Ku Klux Klan, designed to terrorize by the inhuman quality of the costume. Although Spencer finds the coronation less interesting, he does follow several decades of organized protests against the VP Ball by minority groups and their supporters, seeking redress for the exclusion of blacks and working-class people from the power centers of St. Louis. Both of these studies—Davis's and Spencer's—provide the context in which the VP Ball and its bevy of debutantes take on fresh significance.

In the beginning, the Prophets were the Originals, fourteen businessmen who came together in an effort to make their autumn fair a success in the wake of the Great Strike and ongoing labor troubles in St. Louis. Two members of the group, grain brokers Charles and Alonzo Slayback, were former residents of New Orleans. They proposed to buy used floats from the Mysticke Krewe of Comus at a bargain price. These would anchor a gala parade that, depending on the point of view of the observer, was either an intimidating show of force on the part of the city's entrepreneurial class or a terrific attention-getter for St. Louis businesses. Or both.

To fire up interest in the parade, Alonzo concocted a history for the brand-new tradition derived in part from a popular poem called *Lalla Rookh*. This epic potboiler, written by the Irish poet Thomas Moore, was loosely based on the life of an eighth-century Persian trickster named Hashimal-Muganna, a.k.a. the Veiled Prophet of Khursan (or Khorassan). In the 1860s and 1870s, fanciful engravings of Eastern potentates and exotic dancing girls enjoyed wide circulation among gents who collected "naughty" pictures. But by the time the whole, convoluted story had been reworked by several generations of Prophets and GOs (Grand Oracles, or presidents of the group), His Majesty the VP, "a noble potentate" from somewhere in the vicinity of China—or was it Kashmir?—had made it his special mission to bring peace, prosperity, and beauty to the city of St. Louis during an annual levee described in the "Golden Book," a souvenir program issued to the membership in 1928, on the fiftieth anniversary of the first parade.

The parades had been an excellent example of what the Golden Book called "civic leadership incognito." That is, thanks to the anonymous and benevolent Prophets, the annual festival brought spectacle, enjoyment, and edification to the community. The subjects of the dramatic nighttime parades included didactic themes intended to educate the masses and instruct the immigrant. In 1884, for instance, the floats had carried scenes from the plays of Shakespeare. In 1886, "Scenes from American History." As late as 1952, the parade of twenty units depicted important moments in the history of St. Louis (plus the Prophet and his queen). As the decades rolled along, however, the parade subjects grew less earnest on the whole, and the Golden Book itself became more concerned with an accurate record of the queens and their retinue of "special maids of honor." The coronation and the hoopla surrounding it had made the street pageant into little more than an occasion for displaying Her Majesty to the masses in all her royal splendor.

The balls began as invitation-only celebrations of a successful parade, a good fair, and a profitable year. Men were expected to attend in "full dress": white tie, gloves, black swallowtail, vest, etc. The ladies wore their best, minus bonnets, hats, and wraps. The newspapers wrote glowing accounts of the decorations and the dresses. President Cleveland's attendance at the 1887 ball was widely covered and gave St. Louis the advantage in its ongoing rivalry with Chicago for leadership among the western cities. Debutantes were in attendance from the beginning, too, and the girl chosen to dance with the Prophet became "the belle of the ball."

THE BELLE OF THE BALL

The first belle, for 1878, was Miss Susie Slayback, Alonzo's daughter, whose selection was considered a fitting reward for her father's service to the organization. In her own account of the ball, Miss Slayback, writing in the third person, made it clear that the dance was a debutante affair from day one. Since this was quite literally her debut in adult company, she was thrilled to see well-known persons whose names she had heard mentioned at home. The decorations were equally enchanting: songbirds twittering away in cages and a fountain tinkling in the center of the hall. "The society women were exquisitely gowned," she wrote years later, "and the beauty of St. Louis was represented. . . . The time of crowned queens did not come for fourteen years, but the belle of the ball was selected by the Prophet as his most admired partner [and] his selection for the first queen was Miss Susie Slayback. He descended from his lofty seat . . . and escorted her . . . onto the floor where he presented her with a very pretty pearl necklace. Her dress was white satin made with [a] quilted skirt studded with pearl beads and trimmed with lace."

For the first seven years, the names of the belles were as great a secret as the names of the Prophets, in part because women of good breeding did not wish to find themselves mentioned in the press. Nonetheless, just as the debutantes of New York dazzled the public eye and the call-outs of New Orleans evolved into highly publicized debs, St. Louis grudgingly acknowledged the fact that the VP Ball was the first and best coming-out extravaganza in the land specifically conceived to shine a spotlight on the girls in their white raiment. In 1885, Virginia Joy was openly identified as the year's "belle." In 1894, Hester Bates Laughlin was crowned Queen of Love and Beauty in a ceremony that quickly

Carol Lammert Culver, 1957 Veiled Prophet Queen. Missouri Historical Society

began to absorb the ball proper. The parade, too, became a prelude to the crowning, as the Prophet descended from his float and swept into the hall to bestow his favor upon his lady queen.

Miss Laughlin became a semi-celebrity overnight and a symbol of the uppermost crust on the civic pie. When the first *Social Register* was published for St. Louis in 1903, there was the first queen, in all her glory. As Hester had already learned, once a queen, always a queen. In 1928, for the Veiled Prophets' grand anniversary celebration, old ladies were pleased to pose for the papers in the gowns they had worn in 1878. As always, gossips speculated on the identity of the Prophet. But the real question of the hour was who had been chosen as the fiftieth-anniversary queen? It was customary to tell the young lady of her selection well before the appointed hour; over time, a whole host of regulations and obligations made advance planning imperative. In 1902, His Mysterious Self had decreed that queens ought to be both unmarried—putative virgins—and unengaged during their terms. And the winning deb was generally expected to make herself available for the year to perform a growing list of public functions. At the 1928 ball, the outgoing queen, Miss Anne Farrar Semple, paraded into the hall—behind the Prophet, the matrons, the maids of honor, and a brace of heralds and pages—to spontaneous applause. She had been a popular queen. But her day in the spotlight was over.

Now the Prophet called out new names: the maids, in order of preferment, and finally "the fairest maiden of his beloved city, . . . Miss Mary Ambrose Smith," dressed all in white with a train of ermine and gold trailing behind her and a distinctive new diadem upon her head—a band of stones with a spun silver plume standing straight up from the center of the brow. The jeweled finial that held the plume (a synthetic sapphire) was detachable, to be worn ever afterward as a brooch and a mark of honor. The very first VP crown, worn by Hester Bates Laughlin, went on exhibit at the Missouri Historical Society that same week in 1928. A replica of Queen Victoria's crown, it featured a band of pearls and another of ermine, decorated with rubies, emeralds, and diamonds. Miss Laughlin, later Mrs. Carlo Pfister, was deceased, but the crown was a precious family heirloom, proof of her relatives' right to a position of respect in the community. Like their crowns, the debutantes who wore them at the behest of the Veiled Prophet were surrogates for their powerful fathers and their illustrious forebears.

Miss Smith, the newspapers were quick to disclose, was the daughter of a prominent banker, the president of the Mississippi Valley Trust Company. Furthermore, she was descended from Pierre Laclede, founder of the city, on both her mother's and her father's sides. Indeed, the record showed that the new queen was the fourth to claim direct descent from Laclede. Convent educated, the twenty-year-old beauty had recently returned from a year of finishing in Europe. And her cousin, the former Miss Julia Cabanne, had been the 1905 Queen of Love and Beauty. According to the *Post-Dispatch,* "from the exclamations of many old-timers who attended the ball a quarter of a century ago it was apparent that the resemblance between the two was striking."

All in all, Miss Smith was the best the city had to offer, the ideal queen for the Golden Jubilee year. Photographs show a striking brunette, slim, graceful, with a classic flapper hairdo parted in the center and severely pulled back from the face, clutching a bouquet of orchids larger than herself. The formal portraits had been taken in advance and, cloaked in the Prophet's veil of secrecy, released to the papers at the very last minute. After all, what could possibly go wrong between the sitting and the crowning?

Several weeks after the coronation ritual, however, nasty rumors began to circulate. Something was amiss. The queen had returned the crown. She was abdicating. The Prophet, in the words of one horrified observer, "had unwittingly crowned a woman"—not a virtuous maiden. Miss Smith was, in actuality, Mrs. T. C. Birdsall, married in secret two months earlier to a doctor in Winston-Salem, North Carolina. Furthermore, Dr. Birdsall had been divorced in March 1927 in Clayton, Missouri, from his former wife, Martha, who received alimony of $150 a month and custody of Virginia, their two-year-old child. Martha Birdsall had "charged indignities" during the court proceedings, one newspaper gleefully added. Just what those terrible "indignities" were was left to the readers' fevered imaginations.

Mr. Smith apologized to everyone in a tearful statement released on October 11. His daughter had confessed to the marriage three days after the ball, he said. The family had been upset for the past year by the illness of Mary's mother; her father worried that he had failed his daughter in a moment of crisis. But it was his "fondest desire and expectancy that she successfully complete her reign as the Veiled Prophet's Queen." Mr. Smith was devastated by the situation. And so was the Prophet, who decreed the throne vacant for the remainder of the year: "It has been the rule . . . that the Queen . . . be unmarried and that rule has always been observed in the past."

In a 1979 interview, the deposed Miss Smith said that the Prophet gave her some money and told her to leave town, with instructions to register under a false name at hotels along the way. She was finished in the city. Friends turned away. She was never again invited to a VP Ball. Her name was struck from the *Social Register*. Her portrait was removed from the display of queens at the Historical Society. Thomas Spencer asserts that the reason for Mary Smith's draconian punishment was that the queen was supposed to be a model for children—or a sort of pseudo-child herself, subject to the will of her father and the Prophet. Or a true debutante, unwise in the ways of the wicked world and obedient to parental and male authority. This was a difficult position to maintain in the 1920s, when traditional sexual mores were under attack from many quarters. Mary Ambrose Smith's headache-band crown and her short gown marked her as a cousin, at least, of the big-city flapper, a sophisticate—and a woman. A rebel. An independent spirit. A living contradiction of everything the debutante was supposed to be. So she was de-debbed—in effect, denied the right to wear the white satin regalia of maidenhood.

SECRECY AND CIVIC PRIDE

The queen was dead. Long live the queen! And the Veiled Prophet rites hummed along as if nothing untoward had happened. But something had happened: the crash of 1929, which reinforced the need for strong patriarchal leadership. The Veiled Prophet parades depicted the history and heritage of St. Louis, with an emphasis on continuity and stability. The ball itself took on all the trappings of a sanctioned civic event. In 1935, the coronation was moved to the new, publicly owned Kiel Auditorium, where huge crowds could be accommodated in arena-style seating to witness increasingly dramatic crowning rituals. Dancing took a backseat to quasi-Victorian presentation ceremonies, attended by "Bengal Lancers" in exotic makeup and uniforms and the Prophet himself, splendidly robed and duly veiled. No longer a mere adjunct to the parade—the fair had folded years earlier—the ball, with all its fuss and feathers, had become the stepchild of the coronation. First came the matrons, in solemn procession: the ex-queens and maids, with pedigrees rooted in two or three generations of St. Louis society; then

The Veiled Prophet crowning ceremony, 1937. Missouri Historical Society

the "special maids," the also-rans; and finally, the young queen herself, the shining symbol of hope and promise, and a living pledge that all would be well so long as the ruling elite passed its white gowns along from mother to daughter ad infinitum, at the bidding of wealthy and so-licitous fathers.

The press coverage of the Veiled Prophet events during the Great De-pression was no less detailed than it had been in years past, but the focus of interest was now the queen and the social events in which she took the leading role. When Jane Johnson, the 1933 queen, became engaged five years later, the announcement was headline news. Her private debut ball at the St. Louis Country Club was reviewed, along with her parent-age and her exemplary service as queen. At Miss Johnson's coronation, special note had been taken of the former queens in attendance, their subsequent marriages, and their sumptuous attire: they were guarantors, in their furs and jewels, of the city's economic resilience. But it clearly troubled even the society columnists that so many queens had not come back to parade their finery before the city in this, the bleakest year of the depression. The newspapers made a point of tracking down absentees and offering plausible explanations for their defection. A Busch (of the brewing fortune) was still at her summer home in New York State. Mrs. Ness (née Semple) lived in Maryland now. Others were ill or in mourning. Yet it was important to account for the whereabouts of every caryatid who had ever supported the weight of the St. Louis community on her dainty shoulders.

By the mid-1930s, the spotlight also fell on the Queen's Supper, a party (traditionally paid for by her rich father), that had evolved into a post-coronation celebration of her selection. The custom dated back to World War I. The guest list created a kind of elite within the elite, a local version of the hotel suppers featured at eastern debutante balls. In 1933, instead of the usual private parties for the maids and other debs in attendance at the coronation, they were all seated together at a cluster of ten debutantes' tables and feted along with the queen. The supper was another rite of orthodox debbing. The VP festival had now become a fascinating hybrid—the public, civic debut with all the trimmings.

In 1934, when Jane Wells succeeded to the throne of Jane Johnson, publicists fell all over one another in an effort to portray her as "The Perfect Debutante." She wasn't Ziegfeld's American Girl or the ad man's Miss America, they decided. Perfection in a deb was more elusive, more complicated. Lineage counted: Miss Wells's grandfather had been mayor of St. Louis during the famous World's Fair of 1904; her paternal aunt was "one of the loveliest Veiled Prophet's queens ever to grace the throne"; and her older sister had served as a special maid during her own debut year. Jane had gone to the right schools and spent a year abroad. So Miss Wells had "unusual poise and with it a freshness that shows she is completely unspoiled." Enthusiastic. Sincere. Charming. "The Perfect Debutante."

A review of the former queens who planned to attend Miss Wells's coronation noted that they were important symbols of their respective "years." Jean Ford, for instance, would forever be remembered because

Queen Jane Johnson, 1933. Missouri Historical Society

she had been crowned "in those last hysterical hours before the stock market crash of '29." And "already Miss Jane Johnson has become associated in the minds of many of her last year's subjects with the upward swing in the nation's fortunes" after the inauguration of Franklin D. Roosevelt. A queen spoke for the time of her reign, "like the memory of [a] season's most popular song." In St. Louis, history unrolled as an (almost) unbroken litany of prestigious family names—Slayback, Shapleigh, Lambert, Streett, Ferriss, Johnson, Busch, Wells, Chouteau—come good fortune or bad. The melody was sure and steady; only the words of the chorus varied slightly from year to year.

From 1943 to 1945, in deference to the war effort, the Veiled Prophet remained in Khorassan. When he came again, the revived celebration signaled a joyous return to business as usual, peace, and prosperity. The souvenir items traditionally delivered along with invitations to the ball grew more elaborate. The regal purple-and-gold boxes of the postwar years contained items ranging from a spun aluminum porringer emblazoned with the VP crest to cocktail trays and crystal vases and ashtrays similarly marked. Although the queen continued to ride in the parade, now held the evening after the ceremony, it became clear that the two elements were intended to serve different ends. Shortened somewhat, the parade began a long, slow decline into a kiddie affair, with Mother Goose and Disney themes. The coronation now became the center of attention, televised locally beginning in 1949 (and nationally in 1950 and 1951).

Meanwhile, as the fashion industry came out of its wartime slump with Dior's "New Look," the gowns of past queens were reexamined for pedigrees in the salons of Paris and New York, and the current queen's wardrobe was minutely scrutinized. "St. Louis' reigning debutante for 1955" wore a white satin dress designed by her mother. Sally Baker Shepley, the 1952 queen, wore the traditional white tulle in a gown created by Vera, the St. Louis designer. Fashionistas had predicted a rash of designs based on Queen Elizabeth's upcoming coronation, but Queen Sally chose French tulle in honor of the city's historic origins. Queens' courts grew larger as debbing increased in popularity with the return of prosperity. There were more and more gowns to be discussed in mind-numbing detail.

In addition to her crown, the queen was obliged to carry a gigantic bouquet of orchids. How many ways were there to wax poetic over a too-big bunch of flowers? Nonetheless, those flowers were photographed and displayed with the reverence reserved for the royal gown. Little girls flocked to the parade to catch a glimpse of this homegrown queen with her crown and posies, this fairy-tale creature plucked from the same streets they walked. But old-timers complained that the pa-

Sally Baker Shepley, 1952 Veiled Prophet Queen. As fashions change, the plumed crown looks odder and odder. Missouri Historical Society

rade was not what it once was. It used to be glittering and magical, "just like a masquerade ball on wheels," said one aged woman, who had been nine years old at the time of the first parade.

The ball still glittered. On the seventy-fifth anniversary of the first appearance of His Mysterious Majesty, in 1953, antiquarians recalled the

Sought-after VP souvenirs displayed by Miss Anne Collins Taussig, c. 1939. Missouri Historical Society

very first dance—to the music of the "Inaugural Quadrille." The masked gentlemen. The beautiful ladies dressed in their finest. An affair, said the *Globe-Democrat* the next morning, patently superior to Mardi Gras, "as the sunlight is to the moon light." Spectators at the balls of the 1950s began second-guessing the judges, applauding for their favorites. The biggest hand at the 1954 ball went to Miss Whittemore, who curtsied so low that her forehead nearly touched the floor (in a maneuver later known as a "Texas dip"); in light of that feat, her selection as queen met with the enthusiastic approval of the spectators in the upper tiers of seats. The queen mother, it turned out, was a crowd-pleaser herself, remembered for her debutante ball during the 1920s, "one of the most fabulous parties of the day."

IS MISS AMERICA THE NATION'S NUMBER-ONE DEB?

The sports-arena goings-on, with whistles and cheers for the prettiest, gave the coronation the steamy atmosphere of Atlantic City during Miss America week. Begun in the 1920s as a publicity device for the seaside resort, the Miss America Pageant, in its early years, had a Veiled Prophet of its own in the person of King Neptune (who later mutated into longtime MC Bert Parks). But the real business of the pageant was to crown a beauty queen—the ideal American girl. In search of that ideal, both performance (hers) and control (Neptune's, the VP's, Daddy's) were crucial elements, whether the setting was Atlantic City or downtown St. Louis. Frank Deford's groundbreaking study of the Miss America contest suggests that it was a kind of debutante ritual for the masses, requiring competitors to demonstrate poise, grooming, and the genteel accomplishments of maidenhood. The winner—generally the girl in the white dress—got a tiara, a massive spray of roses, and national publicity. In 1957, cool, blonde, blue-eyed Marilyn Van Derbur, Miss Colorado, was dubbed a "debutante" by reporters even before she went on to win the title of Miss America 1958.

To the television audience of young women, argues another analyst of beauty pageants, the contest became a source of knowledge about what one must do to be feminine. Such events also teach the spectator that true American womanhood, like the winner's crown, is accessible to anyone who tries. In fact, the VP coronation was televised for several years before Miss America coverage commenced in 1954; the form if not the content of democratic debbing seems to have originated in St. Louis. Miss America was the Queen of Love and Beauty minus the splendid ancestry. In the 1970s, Miss America often began her reign by riding with the St. Louis queen in the Veiled Prophet parade.

Both spectacles have drawn their share of protest and criticism, too. The Miss America Pageant has been charged with making "whiteness"

Miss America 1948: BeBe Shopp, all-American Girl—and royalty! Minnesota Historical Society

one of the all-American traits required to win the crown; since the 1970s, organizers have headed off public anger by encouraging women of color to enter the contest. In response to ongoing feminist ire, they have suggested that competitors arrive at the pageant committed to a "platform" or social cause to be pursued during the upcoming year. But such advocacy, and the ability to explain one's agenda cogently, will probably not

The queen and her ladies-in-waiting at the 1906 Tournament of Roses, Pasadena, California, as depicted in a later pageant program. First in many social innovations, California helped make debutantes and beauty queens interchangeable.

assuage critics who believe that willful exposure of a woman's person and attributes to scrutiny in a public forum perpetuates her objectification. There is a peculiarly Victorian logic to the position that young women should not parade themselves in the public eye, nor trade upon their charm, good looks, and nice clothes. The debut, as a social institution, was transgressive by nature because it sanctioned such behavior, as does the beauty contest. But all such judgments on the male—or female—gaze fail to reckon with the interests of the would-be queen.

She may well agree to a debut or a spot in the pseudo-monarch's court because of family pressures, but there are many parts of the ritual so pleasurable and enjoyable that dainty arms need not be twisted much. Attention. Applause. The chance to compete, to do one's best. New clothes. The sensual joys of scents and textures and colors. Spectacle. Music. A heady sense of one's own personal power. These experiences, paralleled in many cases by the stimulus provided to young men by sports or even warfare, do not preclude academic accomplishment, a fine character, or career ambitions. Miss America can grow up to be a lawyer, a teacher, a business executive, or a housewife. The Queen of Love and Beauty can do the same.

THE PROPHET UNMASKED

In December 1972, the news on the front page of the *St. Louis Post-Dispatch* was mostly awful. Two B-52s had been shot down near Hanoi: twelve fliers were missing, bringing the total to sixty-seven lost airmen in less than a week. Across the nation women marched for equal rights. Veterans marched in opposition to the war. Neighborhoods marched to protest school busing. In Kansas City, eighty-eight-year-old former president Harry Truman lay near death. On the bright side, the Prophet had come again, and Miss Hope Florence Jones, age nineteen, was his newly crowned queen. In the middle of the ceremony, however, a woman in a formal gown and a red wig slid down a cable from the balcony, crashed to the floor, limped up to the throne, and unmasked His Majesty while a confederate distracted police guards by tossing leaflets from the upper reaches of Kiel Auditorium.

Later, at the supper, guests were all atwitter. Had anybody actually seen the VP—except for a flash of bald pate? Had the "gal" in the wig really shouted "Down with the VP!" as she zoomed toward the stage? Some of the younger attendees thought it was a lark: they had been bored stiff until the mystery lady took her death-defying leap. Old hands were indignant, outraged. "What would these people do if the organization stopped spending money on these events for the city," hissed one matron.

"These people" were Percy Green and his followers, members of AC-TION, or the Action Committee To Improve Opportunity for Negroes, a group described in the *Post-Dispatch* as civil rights militants. As the story spun itself out over the next several days, the paper did not clarify exactly what ACTION had hoped to accomplish by its piece of guerrilla theater. Green said that six of the maids of honor were underground supporters of the protest: "We talked to several of the debutantes this summer and some of them agreed to supply us with tickets to get into the gallery section." Furthermore, around Thanksgiving, ACTION sent a letter to all the debs warning them that a demonstration would take place. But what did Green want? What did ACTION hope to achieve in its series of vocal protests against the Veiled Prophet celebration that began in 1965 (and continued through 1984)?

Green and the other activists demanded economic justice in the form of jobs for minorities. They had chosen the VP Ball to pursue their agenda because it represented wealth, white supremacy, and outright frivolity—and because it had become a semi-official department of white-dominated city government, using public streets, buildings, and services to sustain the existing power structure. A parody of VP pageantry, the street-theater tactics adopted by ACTION were calculated to affect their target audience in a direct, visceral way, at the sites celebrating their most deeply held beliefs. In New York, a group of attention-getting feminists staged a Radical Women's Miss America Protest in 1968, in which they crowned a sheep.

Neither protest killed off the organization under attack. Miss America is still chosen every summer in Atlantic City. And the VP pageant staggered forward as well, albeit in rented quarters and not in Kiel Auditorium. The nighttime parade ended in 1968, replaced by an attenuated Saturday morning event for family viewing. To many, the ball was silly, stupid, and a tasteless display of wealth. ACTION struck again in 1976, spraying tear gas during the coronation. Although the Prophets continued to deny that ACTION had any effect on their policies, black members were finally admitted to the fold in 1979. And that summer the Prophet literally threw in his veil. Instead of a parade, organizers dropped the mysterious name and the costumes in favor of a VP Fair, held on the riverfront on the Fourth of July—a patriotic, civic event featuring nationally known entertainers. The "VP" name was just that: initials, the original meaning of which was all but forgotten.

The VP Fair—later Fair St. Louis—was subject to the same racial tensions that had plagued the ball. Whites and blacks scuffled in the streets. The city was charged with spending public money on an event led by a mostly white oligarchy. The fair lost money and, like many similar downtown festivals of the past half century of suburbanization, its future was always in doubt. But through it all, the coronation survived, albeit in the velvet underground of a hotel ballroom as a private, members-only event. Every December, college sophomores come home for Christmas vacation and "come out" at the ball. They claim, as they adjust their tiaras, that it is really an honor for Daddy—a symbolic crowning of the local elite by itself, the last gasp of ancestor worship in the modern Midwest.

Throughout the 1970s, eligible maidens had testily declined to endorse the hoopla. When he declared that "they are being auctioned off to white society" in a not-so-subtle form of slavery, Percy Green struck a nerve. He did, as he would often claim, have his supporters in the debs' own ranks. "Elitism is wrong!" declared one pretty rebel in a ball gown. "The young are so earnest these days," cooed a tactful social secretary. "They all want to change the world." A 1970 maid of honor was blunt: "This is such a farce! This kind of exhibitionism has got to go." A 1971 maid called the ball "much ado about nothing. I don't plan to have my daughter in it!" The good (or bad) old days, when fathers put themselves up for membership in the Veiled Prophets on the night their first daughter was born, were over. New mothers no longer phoned the St. Louis Country Club from the maternity ward to reserve a date for a reception and dance to celebrate their newborn daughters' future coronations. The days of newspaper interviews, television shows, and parade floats ended in 1979. But the debbing, of course, goes on, and on, and on.

f debuts are about social distinction, then what was a leading Washington hostess of the late 1930s to make of a newly hired "colored" cook who warned the lady of the house to expect some absenteeism: "I'll have to ask you for lots of my evenin's off, Ma'am," she says in the dialect that passed for good-natured racial humor in the prewar era. "You see, I'se a debutante this year." But largely ignored by white socialites, African-Americans have been coming out at lavish balls of their own for generations. For every black girl slighted by the selection committee of an Old Guard cotillion, a hundred more have bowed to the high society of their own communities, under rules that often favor achievement and promise over wealth and lineage.

HIGH SOCIETY IN BLACK AMERICA

This is not to say, of course, that old families of distinction are lacking among African-Americans. Some of the best-known clans trace their roots back to Napoleon, to the family of Martha Washington, to the descendants of renowned American painter Henry O. Tanner. But what is most prized is success in the here and now, especially in business and the professions. Before integration, the elite class among blacks was relatively small, limited to the few who managed to obtain an education and its attendant benefits: teachers, pastors, doctors, dentists, funeral directors. With increased career options, the number of those active in the kinds of clubs and philanthropic causes liable to sponsor debuts has increased dramatically. Jack and Jill of America, one of the defining organizations for the families of black professionals, was founded in 1938, when the comic-operetta cook quoted above was rehearsing for her debut. Along with the Links, the Deltas, and the Alpha Kappa Alphas

(AKAs), Jack and Jill chapters continue to sponsor debuts for high school seniors.

Nonetheless, "Negro" society was an all but invisible ripple in the main current of American culture until the first stirrings of the civil rights movement alerted the mass media to the existence of pretty black debs. *Life* magazine led the way, with its pictorial coverage of a Harlem cotillion in 1950. *Life*, to be sure, had always loved a party: from the time of its founding in 1936, Henry Luce's picture magazine had deliberately assumed the sequined mantle of society reportage. So readers were given a front-row seat at all kinds of social events, affording them a glimpse of the exotic world of the rich and famous, as well as the universal human emotions shared by anyone marking a milestone in life with a gala observance. People saw how the other half lived—how various minorities, ranging from millionaires to black jitterbuggers in Harlem, were like and unlike themselves. Nor were the editors entirely uncritical of what they observed. In January 1937, in one of *Life*'s many deb stories, the text actually questioned the wisdom of a local plutocrat spending $55,000 on a debut in Philadelphia's Bellevue-Stratford ballroom during hard times, when that sum amounted to the annual income of twenty average American workers.

Life's coverage of the Harlem Cotillion of 1950 helped disclose the existence of a vibrant social world that defied the racial stereotypes purveyed by segregationists. The April ball, attended by almost five thousand guests, was a model of decorum. Fifty-two young women were presented, each one dressed in traditional white (with pearls), each one sponsored by a civic or social club that demanded proof of an "acceptable" family background. Escorts chosen for the debs were all college men of impeccable reputation. And the evening began with the grand entrance of the founder of the event, a prominent black matron, on the arm of Grover Whalen, "Mr. New York," the dapper, white, gent-about-town who was the city's semi-official greeter, now board chairman of Coty, Inc. Coty, long a sponsor of the best Manhattan debutante functions, presented each Harlem deb with a bottle of perfume.

Life quoted Harlem's *Amsterdam News*, which described the festivities as "an overwhelming success" marked by "unusual excitement and picturesque splendor." Indeed, the party went on until 3 A.M. Profits from the sale of tickets and programs amounted to a whopping $9,082, destined for local welfare agencies. And the photos were precisely those ritualized images used for all deb balls: a formal portrait of a small group of debutantes looking solemn and self-conscious; a group shot, with lines of girls and boys facing each other at the conclusion of a figure dance; nervous debs primping behind the scenes; and clumps of jittery escorts, stoic and stiff in their tail suits.

But two additional photos differed from the norm. One showed a formidable row of conservatively dressed older ladies watching the proceedings with evident anxiety: these were the organizers and committee members who screened the debs and paired them with proper escorts. The other depicted their opposite numbers—the fez-wearing gentlemen patrons of Brooklyn's Eureka Shrine Temple No. 10, who had sponsored the appearance of the daughter of a member of the group's women's auxiliary. Unlike the kinds of "proud papa" or "well-dressed grande dame" pictures always taken at contemporary white debuts, these phalanxes of attentive elders demonstrated that their debs were going into the world with the blessing, the backing, and the whole-hearted approval of their community.

Although parents played a comparatively minor role in the Harlem debut of 1950, an exception could always be made in the case of a black superstar's seventeen-year-old daughter. In November 1961, Cookie (Carol) Cole, eldest child of singer Nat "King" Cole, prepared to make her debut at the Links Cotillion in Los Angeles. She was a bundle of nerves as *Ebony* magazine followed her through the last-minute preparations, under the watchful eye of little sister Sweetie (Natalie). Cookie was sure she would fall down the stairs during the introduction, drop her bouquet, put a run in her nylons as she made her bow or "reverence" to the crowd, spill something on her beautiful princess-line gown of white silk, or worse, despite all the practices and fittings and preparations. The latter included a series of deb luncheons at which Links members polished their charges' manners and deportment, and gabfests with other debs on important issues of the day. For Cookie, the burning issue was boys: the cotillion was her first date, and her escort was a college man!

But an even greater challenge awaited Cookie and the five hundred Links socialites gathered at the Beverly-Hilton Hotel. Because he had an earlier engagement to perform at a dinner, Nat was anxious about arriving at the Hilton in time to walk his daughter through her grand entrance and bow. Much to the surprise of Cookie and the rest of the crowd, however, he brought the President of the United States along with him. The dinner had been held in honor of John F. Kennedy, who was staying at the Hilton. Could he drop in on the ball, Kennedy wondered? "Nat sang at our dinner tonight, so I thought I'd reciprocate. I'm grateful to you girls for letting an itinerant President come and visit your party." Before he left, the President found Cookie Cole and told her that she looked just beautiful.

The *Life* magazine of middle-class black America, *Ebony* presented Cookie's debut as a routine matter made extraordinary by her unexpected guest. If race was the subtext, the presidential visit was the focus of the article. But throughout the 1960s, coverage of debuts and the organizations that sponsored them became a staple of *Ebony*'s avid coverage of black social life. In the spring of 1962, for example, the spotlight fell on the Eighth Kansas City Cotillion, which presented twenty-eight girls (out of fifty applicants) under the joint auspices of the Kansas City, Kansas, and Kansas City, Missouri, chapters of the Alpha Kappa Alpha sorority. According to the members, scholastic achievement counted. The affair, said one source, "makes prospective debutantes strive for better grades to be accepted." Nonetheless, despite the emphasis on scholarship, the families of the debs were "from middle to higher income brackets." And although no commitments were demanded, the ball aimed to inspire debutantes to join AKA chapters on their respective campuses.

FORMING GOOD CHARACTER WITH WHITE DEB DRESSES

In Oklahoma City, the ladies of the Nu Vista Club admitted that the tradition of the East Coast debut was a "relatively new departure for Negro socialites." But in the fall of 1962, Nu Vista was presenting its fifth crop of debs to an audience of two thousand spectators. The funds raised went for scholarships. Yet the event itself centered less on scholastic matters than on lineage and money. Here, the emphasis fell on the mothers and fathers of the college girls chosen to participate. "It's the community's way of telling parents—'You have done a magnificent job of rearing your daughter' and to the debs—'We are proud of you,'" said the club's president. The ball, which followed the usual pattern of presentations, bows, and figure dancing, concluded with a kind of beauty pageant in which a queen, a "Miss Personality," and a "Miss Congeniality" were crowned. The quality of the gowns, all from "better shops," clearly enhanced the competitive prospects of would-be royalty.

In the prosperous postwar years, then, African-Americans—like their white counterparts—celebrated a whole range of middle-class ideals through debutante balls: family, decorum, dress, preparation for future positions of social leadership. They also celebrated the attainment of the financial means necessary for snapping up designer ball gowns and bouquets. While the fabled East Coast cotillions cloaked themselves in philanthropic causes to dispel charges of extravagance and waste, however, the majority of the black ceremonies maintained their ties to education, acknowledging that the attainment of a degree was the surest steppingstone to economic security and social acceptance.

The First Telstar Cotillion, sponsored by the Salem Methodist Church of Harlem in 1963, is a case in point. *Ebony* went to the dance and witnessed the Grand March, the first waltz, the choreographer's backstage instructions, and the coronation of the queen (who earned the honor by selling the most tickets to the spectators' gallery in the Roosevelt Hotel ballroom). The funds raised were slated for scholarships. The twenty debs, or "belles of the ball," were college freshmen or college-bound high school seniors. The queen waltzed away with a $300 grant for tuition at the school of her choice.

The Ninth Cotillion Ball of the Links chapter of Oakland, California, in 1965 featured twenty-seven debutantes, singled out for scholarship, leadership, and the desire to continue their education. The twenty-seven debs corresponded to the twenty-seven members of the local club, each of whom agreed to sponsor a young woman. So, as *Ebony* noted, "an industrious girl from a meager background may suddenly find herself projected into society." The cause for which the proceeds were intended was the NAACP's Legal Defense and Educational Fund. The by-product was the education of twenty-seven young women of promise. The leader of Zeta Phi Beta's North Carolina chapter, opening its fourteenth annual deb ball in 1964, said that this was the "time when we can do two important things: prove that it's not only the very wealthy girl who can have a fine coming-out, and bring in more funds for hospitals, libraries,

Miss Nia Reid is presented to society at the Cotillion Ball, Detroit, 1995. Detroit Free Press

scholarships and other projects. It's not just a grand party; it's a party with a purpose." Still, although the girls were expected to complete their education with a boost from Zeta, their escorts were also beneficiaries of the ball. The college boys had a chance to meet "a whole new generation of young marriageables," noted one of the "sorors" observing the ceremonial minuet that began the evening. Beneath all the high-minded rhetoric, the planning, and the rituals, debbing still came down to the fundamental fact that here was a tenderly nurtured bud with all the qualifications to make a fine wife for a suitable gentleman.

Within the black community, some have criticized debuts for copying a sexist and paternalistic white ritual that is outmoded. Some argue that the emphasis on professional credentials and social standing only serves to ghettoize have-nots in the ranks of African-Americans. Others point out that since the postwar formation of black groups sponsoring deb balls, the barriers to black participation in all-white coming-out extravaganzas have begun to fall. In the early 1980s, for instance, an African-American debutante—Candace Bond—became the first woman of color to make her bow at the Veiled Prophet Ball. But is integration a good thing when the issue is the presentation of one's child to the society in which she will be expected to live and work? Don't black-and-white debuts essentially funnel off the most talented and ambitious teens, consigning them to the ranks of white society? Is all-black high society any less insular than the clannishness of the white elite? Are separate-but-equal social arrangements preferable to tokenism? Should young black women be encouraged to think about social ambition at a time when academic achievement ought to be paramount?

Detroit, and especially the wealthy suburbs of the city, has a history of wildly expensive debuts going back to at least 1907, when *Detroit Saturday Night* began to chronicle the balls in a special "Debutante Issue." The local custom was to begin the season with teas, at which the deb would be introduced formally to her mother's friends. At a later date, she met male society at an individual ball often held at the plush Detroit Athletic Club or the Grosse Pointe Yacht Club. The servants at these galas were, of course, black. In 1949, a newly formed African-American Cotillion Club began to plan for its first ball, in the prevailing Detroit manner. The ball, in other words, was a male-dominated function. And despite its name and its best-known public event, the Cotillion Club has been an active political organization, agitating for change in the greater Detroit area. The ball, as a result, is sometimes viewed as a mere afterthought, although the pages of Detroit's leading black newspaper, the *Michigan Chronicle*, suggest that Cotillion Club debs have helped the group exercise its political clout through their ability to attract favorable publicity. The club, in turn, has been careful to showcase the character, volunteerism, career goals, and good grades of its chosen ladies.

The Cotillion Ball's printed program for 1953 opened with a discussion of the causes to which the club planned to direct its efforts for the year. These included a drive to admit black members to the local auto club (AAA), taking legal action in the case of discriminatory practices by local businesses, and a major voter registration drive. The official history of the Cotillion Club, prefacing later editions of the dance program, attributed its formation to rampant discrimination in Detroit housing after World War II, coupled with blatant racism in the police and fire departments. The debutante ball raised funds to support legal and political action in these areas. But potential debs were also trained in leadership and encouraged to spearhead community action campaigns. *Cotillion News*, published fitfully in the 1950s, supported black candidates for important city positions, including seats on the school board, and celebrated the election of members to key positions in the NAACP, whose membership drives were vigorously supported by the club.

The black debutante, then, finds herself in a highly ambiguous situation. Whether she likes it or not, debbing is a politically charged issue, especially for an African-American minority still in search of a satisfactory relationship to the dominant majority. Organizations like the Cotillion Idlewild of Dallas, Texas, founded in the 1920s by black professional men of the city, cling to an older model of service: in order to promote the value of education, they choose their debs on the basis of intellectual achievement. Modeled on an exclusive all-white men's club of the same name, the Idlewilds acknowledge their origins while celebrating their originality in turning the debut to more serious ends: "We copied from the white group at the beginning," a former president admitted, "but it's not a copy any more!"

The chairwoman of the Ladies' Selection Committee, in a 1951 article entitled "Why We Need the Debutante Ball," stated that every girl deserved her moment in the "glitter and glamor" of the social spotlight, whatever her economic status. She also touched indirectly on the legacy of slavery, in which women were often treated as sexual chattel. "The Cotillion Debutante Ball was designed to stimulate a desire in the young women of Detroit to maintain good moral character regardless of station. . . . The Cotillion men in this project show appreciation for the high standards which our girls maintain."

BEAUX: BOY DEBS

Given the Cotillion Club's political activism and male membership, it is no surprise that the cotillions soon began to pay a corresponding attention to Detroit boys on the brink of manhood. An anomalous feature of the Cotillion Club Ball was the prominence of the debs' escorts. Throughout the 1990s, the typical dance program devoted a page to each deb and her date, listing the vital statistics of both: age, high school and organizational activities, planned college major, sponsor, presenter. By 2000, the year of the fifty-first ball, escorts were being put through a rigorous course of training in manners before the big night, and the selection of a "Mr. Congeniality" had become a high point of the evening. If a debutante ball could change the lives and aspirations of the women of Detroit, could it not also work its magic on the young men? On the future leaders of the Cotillion Club?

A recent study of the Young Gentlemen's Beautillion in Waterloo, Iowa, locates the male equivalent of the debutante cotillion. The sponsor is the Black Alliance, an organization for African-American professional men dedicated to what W. E. B. DuBois called "uplift," or the improvement of the community through education and strong leadership. In keeping with this mission, the members themselves play a starring role in the formalities. That is, they are introduced before the young men they have mentored, and their job affiliations are read out with their biographies. The "beaux" whom they are sponsoring come last, walking down a runway with panache and personal style. Although a somber tux is the uniform of the day, participants use hairstyle and gesture to play up to the audience, as if they were contestants in a male beauty pageant.

Beaux's escorts or dates often wear black gowns, to match the tuxedos, in a deliberate inversion of the debutante costume (just as Bette Davis, playing a Southern belle, wears red in the 1938 tear-jerker *Jezebel*). At many all-white balls, too, the debs of the past year—the post-debs—wear black. The symbolism seems obvious: in contrast to the virginal white of the classic debutante gown, the black dress signifies a greater sophistication, even a touch of sexiness. And that seems to be the message of the beaux's ball. If these are the young men of the community, then it is appropriate to pair them with young women—not starry-eyed girls. Surely, the white dress once meant what it did in bridal attire; namely, that the wearer was an innocent. In a modern-day context, however, white seems to stand for virtue of a more generalized sort. The female in white is proclaiming her attainments and her potential as a future member of the adult community. She is, in effect, a blank slate, while her sister in black has already accepted the burden of adult maturity and responsibility.

It is tempting to trace this mode of self-presentation back to the African-American parades of the nineteenth century or to the jazz funerals of twentieth-century New Orleans, with their fancy steps and strutting. Although manuals like E. M. Woods's *The Negro in Etiquette* (1899) urged restraint in dress and body movement, the better to emulate white masculinity, musicologists have recently proposed that the cotillion itself—the elaborate figure dance with its exaggerated gestures—may have been developed by black musicians in the early 1800s to express their particular dramatic penchant. "When we use the word 'Ladies,'" wrote Mr. Woods, "it is generally understood by colored people to mean white women." But in our own era, a strut and a spin can signal the arrival of a distinct African-American individual, entitled to the interest and respect of his community. These are the marks of beau-dom. This young fellow is a man!

For the most part, despite a long tradition of coming out in the black community, the custom is not well known outside the confines of that racial group. The Bachelor-Benedicts Ball in Washington, D.C., dates back to 1910. The Tuxedo Ball, in the same city, attracts debs and dates from all over the country. The Ball of Roses cotillions put on by local chapters of the Girl Friends organization are also national in scope. But these have seldom been matters of interest to the mainstream media. That situation changed abruptly in 1994, with the publication of John Berendt's best-seller, *Midnight in the Garden of Good and Evil*. Set in Savannah, Georgia, this documentary account of a famous murder and trial of the 1980s includes a chapter contrasting an annual society party held by the defendant on the night before the cotillion ball with the black deb ball scheduled for the same evening.

SEGREGATION AND COTILLIONS

The Alpha Cotillion, sponsored by the Alpha Phi Alpha fraternity's graduate organization, has been staged in Savannah since 1945. Berendt's informant, the founder of the ball, stresses the good character of the debutantes and their educational goals: to be an Alpha deb, a girl needs to have graduated from high school and matriculated at an institution of higher learning. In addition, candidates are required to attend "Charm Week," under the supervision of the wives of the Alphas, the Alphabettes. The ball, Berendt learned, was seldom covered by the local press with the detail or intensity accorded the white cotillion. It was only in the 1960s, for example, that the *Savannah Morning News* began to publish the names of black debs and to accord courtesy titles—Miss, Mr., Mrs.—to African-Americans. But the Alphas have contented themselves with the certainty that their ball is far better than the cotillion; it is their girls—not the snooty Southern belles—who dance the ancient minuet flawlessly!

In the 1997 Clint Eastwood (director) film based on the book, Berendt's evening at the Alpha Cotillion is the gaudy high point of a subplot involving the antics of a black female impersonator who makes periodic appearances to tweak the pretensions of Savannah society, both black and white. "The Lady Chablis" crashes the dance in full drag, fondles the handsomest escorts, and casts aspersions on the characters of the prettiest debs, thereby calling the efficacy of the whole ritual into question. Chablis seems indifferent to issues of black versus white, since she is an outcast from virtually every segment of Savannah society. Exclusivity, pretension, sham: it is superior airs that irk her, no matter who adopts them. Debbing strikes her as hurtful or, worse, silly.

Whitney Terrell's highly praised novel *The Huntsman* (2001) approaches the same subject from a different angle. A white deb, daughter of an influential Kansas City judge, is found floating in the Mississippi. As the story explores the circumstances of her murder, the police go back to the Founders Ball—a.k.a. the Jewel Ball—to which the victim had invited a black man. His rage against the racial divisions in the city is the real focus of the book. The ball, writes Terrell, "ostensibly a benefit for the museum, was in fact the sanctioned and celebrated attempt on the part of white society to repeal time, an effort both mythic and bizarre in scale. . . . [When] the fathers presented their daughters to the city, they were really offering up their flesh to them. . . . [T]he Founders Ball had never had a debutante who was black." And the gallant escort of the white socialite-in-training was a handsome black beau whose assertion of manhood was brutally rejected by the Kansas City establishment.

In June 1995, an article in the *Detroit Free Press* took up the matter of black debs and escorts as if the newspaper had just discovered their existence. The staff writer followed the evening with several young couples at the forty-sixth Cotillion Debutante Ball, from the practices to the Cinderella march down a runway, to the presentation and bow, to sleepy debs taking off their high heels and finding their way home. The customs, it seemed, were not materially different from those of the lavish balls of yesteryear mounted by millionaire automakers bent on dynastic glory: the white dress, the curtsy, the gloves, the flowers. But there were several key deviations from local custom. First, both debs and escorts were required to practice every Sunday for twelve weeks before the big night. Subjects included waltzing and bowing, but other topics were also addressed—career planning, "social awareness," dressing for success, etiquette. And the preparations were topped off by a talent tea at which each deb performed for the group, demonstrating poise and self-confidence. Second, wealth was no prerequisite for participation. The club selected the young men and women and assumed most of the cost. Finally, the debut was one step on the road to college and adulthood, but only one small, mostly enjoyable dance step, performed to perfection.

White buds of the 1960s had debbed 'til they dropped. Survivors told the *Free Press* that they wouldn't do it again for love or money. A yearlong pain. Too ostentatious, said a woman whose father had arranged for the Supremes to entertain at her private ball. Too old-fashioned, too corny, said a rich Detroit twenty-year-old: formality was *so* over! "I would be embarrassed to have a deb ball." Besides the Cotillion Club's dance, the only other serious deb parties going on in Detroit in those days had to do with race, ethnicity, religion, or a combination thereof. There was the Viennese Strauss Ball put on by the Austrian Society, the Presentation Ball of the United Christian Lebanese Association, the Quince Años parties held among Latino families on the southwest side—even the Jewish bat mitzvah, celebrating the female coming of

age. Debbing had transmuted itself into an expression of cultural differences and pride in those deviations from the all-American, white-
bread norm.

The nineteenth-century coming-out tea and the twentieth-century
blowout at the Waldorf were all about differences, too. Debs were shown
to be members of a certain social caste, rich enough to keep up with the
Vanderbilts and the Astors. Or determined enough to hire press agents
to plant their names in gossip columns, as habitués of the best tables at
the Stork Club. Debs were the marriageable little girls of indulgent daddies who could spoil them rotten—and then purchase true-blue husbands for them from the best available stock. Even when deb balls
donned the sackcloth of charity, the criteria for debbing remained exclusive, in the sense of being exclusionary. To exclude is to define and
to herald one's own superiority. Using that logic, however, any club or
group that admits some, but not others—all societies that adopt uniforms and rituals—is probably suspect: everybody from the Catholic
Church to the Cub Scouts and the Marine Corps. But as American society
has became more and more diverse, Catholics and African-Americans
and Polish-Americans and even the Marines (a military ball puts most
deb parties to shame!) have insisted on their own worth by colonizing
rites of passage that speak to their pride, heritage, and sense of entitlement. Hence the Gotham Ball for New York's Catholic debs, once segregated from the Anglo-Saxon Protestant mainstream. Hence the Cotillion Club Ball for black women. And the revival of the quinceañera, or
coming-of-age ceremony newly popular in Hispanic and Latino communities across the country.

QUINCEAÑERA

The origins of the qinceañera (quince for short)—a gala celebration
of a girl's fifteenth birthday—are obscure. Some say that it is an ancient
Aztec initiation rite taken over by the Catholic Church in the sixteenth
century. Or a ceremony begun in the nineteenth century by Carlota, the
Austrian Empress of Mexico and the Duchess of Alba, on the model of
European court debuts. Many American clergy pressured into opening
a daylong and highly secular quinceañera with a religious service maintain that it is no more than an invented tradition, liable to bankrupt the

"Mis Quince Años" dressed for her big day. Catalogs of gowns and accessories give the young lady images to dream by.

family of the girl so honored; to them, it is a wanton display of material wealth and procreative potential that ought not be sanctioned by the church.

However, anthropologists doing fieldwork in remote villages in the Andes have encountered similar ceremonies for both girls and boys, signaling their readiness for marriage. In preparation for the party, the teenagers are expected to act like adults by performing good works in the community and in the church. Tourists and vacationers have come upon "Mis Quince Años" observances, complete with white dress and tiara, all over rural Latin America and Cuba. Until the 1960s, however, the quinceañera was rare among Latin populations eager to assimilate quietly into suburban America. Or the ritual was absorbed into look-alike debuts: in Chicago, the Cordi-Marian Cotillion; in El Paso, the Symphony Debut; in Zapata County, Texas, the Quinceañera Ball.

In its most highly developed recent form, the American quinceañera leaves conventional debuts in the shade. Except for Cubans and Puerto Ricans, who have discarded most of the religious portions of the ceremony, the day begins with a Mass or a blessing at which the young woman renews her baptismal vows and commits herself to a virtuous adult life. Often she comes to church dressed as a bride, in a long white gown. The bell-shaped skirts favored for the occasion are thought to reflect Spanish court dress of the imperial past. Accompanying the *quinceañera* to church are relatives, who present her with a religious medal and a Bible or prayer book, and members of her official retinue: a *chambelán* (also known as the *galán* or the *escorte*), who can be a father, a brother, or an out-and-out date; a court of honor composed of fourteen young couples, who stand for the years of her life (a half-court will do just as well to maintain the symbolism); and godparents, along with other *padrinos* and *madrinas* who have made material contributions to the festivities. If a church service is held, it is often climaxed by a dressing ritual in which the girl's mother puts a tiara or crown on her head while her father removes her flats and replaces them with the high-heeled shoes of womanhood.

These semi-sacramental components of the quinceañera can also be folded into a reception or party organized along the lines of a debut grafted onto a Broadway musical, a senior prom, and a dream wedding. In addition to the redressing of the *quinceañera*, the *chambelán* or a hired

Special "must-have" items for a proper quinceañera include a scepter, a tiara, and Spanish-language greeting cards.

MC introduces the other members of the court and the young lady of the hour, who curtsies to the guests and opens a series of dances: rehearsed numbers performed by the court and the kinds of girl-and-father, mother-and-date ballroom dancing—the *vals*, or waltz—associated with wedding receptions. This activity takes place in a lavishly decorated room often featuring stage sets made or rented for the evening: arbors, Cinderella coaches, giant seashells, or a wicker peacock throne enhanced with lace, ribbons, and artificial flowers, where she sits for the shoe exchange. There are toasts, thank-yous to the sponsors, and a response from the *quinceañera* in which she expresses gratitude for her upbringing. A dinner and a less formal dance, with a DJ, and everyone joining in. There are printed programs, listing the sponsors and their offerings. A multi-tiered cake embellished with statuary and fountains. Favors for the guests in the form of *capias* (ribbons) or *cerámicas* (figurines). A satin-covered photo album. A ceremonial pillow on which the birthday girl may kneel at church; if the service is omitted, the pillow can be used to present each of the traditional gifts—earrings, a bracelet, a medal or necklace, the crown, a bouquet, and so forth. Elaboration of the symbolic gifts speaks to a growing prosperity among those of Latin heritage. The objects themselves, available from professional, paid planners, may have originated in the markets of Guadalajara, from which many of the costly, brand-new "traditional" aspects of the rite are said to come.

The gaudiest, six-figure quinceañeras are held among the Cuban exiles of Miami. Girls have been known to drop into swimming pools from helicopters at the moment of introduction. Dance numbers performed by the *damas* and their partners are choreographed by experts and perfected for months on end. Nothing is too good, too big, too expensive for the fifteen-year-old daughter of the house. The age at which the ritual is enacted may be the most traditional thing about a modern-day quince, although even here, Mexican-American families have begun to hold "Sweet Sixteen" parties using the same props and iconography. So this is clearly meant to be a teenage rite of passage, something like the old-style debut tea that marked the completion of a girl's domestic education. But throughout the later twentieth century, the age of the average debutante crept upward to accommodate college plans: maturity, in Anglo society, was deferred longer and longer, until the debut itself became laughably redundant. After her presentation, the *quinceañera* can act like a woman. She can date, wear makeup, take responsibility for many of her own decisions. In the social climate of today's America, to be sure, she has already done most of these grown-up things before the magic age of fifteen. But the choice of fifteen as the symbolic moment of transition masks parental fears that their teenager may lose her virtue as well as her home-taught values in the permissive ambience of a Phoenix or a Fort Worth high school. An unsuccessful movement to develop a quince for boys was organized in the 1970s to prevent them from joining criminal gangs.

In the preference for a teen debut, Latinos—like African-Americans—acknowledge the threat posed to the young by mass culture and the loosening of family bonds. But unlike black debuts, in which the emphasis falls squarely on education and betterment, the quinceañera aims to legitimate and control the sexuality of the pubescent girl. She is ready to

"Mis Quince" is captured in all the perfection of the moment in a doll to be treasured for years to come.

be a wife, a sexual being, says the bridal regalia. She is grown-up and a member of a successful clan that is able to shower her with jewelry, finery, limos, and all manner of pretty, feminine souvenirs of her big day. She is Cinderella, off to the ball. No wedding could be quite as wonderful: then, she will have to share the spotlight with the groom! The arguments of a fretful clergy opposed to the ruinous extravagance of the quinceañera, the celebration of biological maturity, and the overt sexual promise of many facets of the ceremony are probably valid. So is their belief that this is a synthetic, inauthentic ritual. But none of these objections cuts to the heart of debbing or quincing: honoring oneself and one's female offspring and giving mothers, who are in charge of such happenings, the chance to validate their lives, their maternity, and the power that the bloom of youth uniquely accords to girls at this time of life.

The case for an intense level of maternal involvement is similar to defenses of beauty pageants for children in the wake of the Jon Benét Ramsey murder case. Indeed, many of the same mall shops and Internet retailers that supply quinceañera finery for fifteen-year-olds also purvey all the accessories needed to transform a five-year-old into a miniature version of Miss America. And it cannot be coincidental that the venues in which the quinceañera thrives—the border states and the warm-weather South—are also prime spawning grounds for big-time pageant culture. Many of the "inauthentic" aspects of the quince come straight from the world of the beauty contest: a staged show, "theme" parties with semi-professional dance routines, tiaras ("Just like Princess Diana's!" reads one ad; "Just like Audrey Hepburn!"), high heels, big hair, and a sparkly white dress.

Every one of the competitors in the 2001 Miss America Pageant, televised live from Atlantic City, wore a white, fairy-tale gown for the opening introductions. For the "evening-wear" competition, the twenty semifinalists, most still in white, were led to the stage by a father or a brother to make a formal bow to the audience. If the beauty pageant is a democratic, mass-media coming out, then the Miss America contest, since 1921, has been crowning the nation's designated Deb of the Year— or our prettiest, peppiest *quiceañera*. Even in swimsuits, most pageant contestants still wear their ceremonial high heels.

Although the Misses America can be counted on to entertain troops and avoid seditious comments to the press, they are not primarily in-

The lovely Queen of the Rose
Tournament, Barbara Dougall,
and the six Maidens of Her
Court. Left to right: Eleanor Wennerberg,
Gladys Hadley, Peggy Lou Anderson, Miss
Dougall, Bernice Mongreig, Roberta Scott
and Peggy Lynn Ingham, in regal gowns.

The 1939 Rose Queen and the "maidens" of her court pictured in the souvenir program of the Tournament of Roses that year. Although the dresses do not seem especially "Latin," that was the year's theme!

volved with perpetuating or honoring the American heritage. But the quinceañera, whatever its importations from movie and pageant land, is about having Latino or Hispanic ancestry. Even the most assimilated high school sophomore, in this one rite of passage, acknowledges her ethnicity. Ethnic pride is another legacy of the civil rights movement of the 1960s: the quince, and other hyphenated celebrations, grew in popularity as it became socially viable to admit to "different" geographic origins, menus, customs, and ideals. Insofar as those ideals include premarital chastity and eventual motherhood for girls, the quinceañera accurately portrays old-country expectations, even as they come under increasing pressure from contemporary culture at large. Quincing is about retaining respect for the old ways, even if they are sometimes honored in startling new forms.

One of ironies of life in Texas, on the permeable Mexican border, is the turnabout appropriation of Latino culture by well-to-do Anglos. The civic debut rituals of San Antonio are a good example of make-believe Mexicanism, which is also an essential part of California festival life, including the Santa Barbara Fiesta and the Tournament of Roses Parade in Pasadena. In San Antonio, a Battle of the Flowers Parade inaugurated in 1891 spawned the Fiesta, which, like the Veiled Prophet celebrations in St. Louis, eventually became the exclusive purview of white debs of good family. The distinctive mark of the Fiesta queen (and her numerous attendants) is a custom-made court robe that trails to fantastic lengths and is decorated in giant embroidered patterns enriched with glass jewels and/or tiny mirrors, all the better to glitter under artificial light. The gowns are so heavy and stiff that debs often need to be transported to their runway in an open-bed pickup. In addition, San Antonio Coronation debutantes disappoint the crowd unless—robe and all—they perform that infamous "Texas dip" in which the lady's forehead actually grazes the floor, in imitation of Pavlova's pose at the end of the second act of *Swan Lake*.

Columnist Molly Ivins, sharp-tongued chronicler of all things Texan, observed that the overwhelming too-muchness of the San Antonio Fiesta has cast its spell over all types of comings out in that state. "Texas debutantes are like Las Vegas or a thousand-pound cheese or a submarine sandwich as long as a football field," she wrote in 1991. "Doesn't matter whether you like it or not—you have to admit that it's really something. Even if you can't define what." So Texas families, going Detroit tycoons of an earlier day one better, see nothing amiss in hiring civic auditoriums and complete circuses to entertain at their daughters' coming-out parties. Likewise, at a good, new-fashioned Texas quinceañera, no quantity of baubles and furbelows and fripperies is too excessive for the moment when the little *niña* becomes a full-blown bride-to-be. Whether the debutante is black, white, brown, rich, working class, a college girl, or a bright-eyed high school kid bent on a career in local politics, her moment in the limelight ought to be "really something." Fluffy. Glitzy. Buoyant. Odd. An event to remember, even if you can't quite grasp what happened.

*I*t's a balmy spring night: moon glow, soft breezes, a twelve-passenger limo with a light-up neon bar. Powder-blue tail suits. A sprinkling of opera hats and canes. Slinky dresses. Big fluffy gowns. Corsages and boutonnieres with that wet, garden smell that cuts right through the scent of the muskiest perfumes. Long, uncomfortable silences broken by squeals of delight as each new couple joins the caravan bound for the gym. The gym? No. Tonight it's Paris— a homemade Eiffel Tower holding up a cheesecloth ceiling with electric twinkle stars (a.k.a. last year's Christmas lights). Punch bowls. Chaperones. Cheesy favors. A professional photographer off in one corner, setting up an archway of tired paper roses to frame his subjects. Dinner for two beforehand at a white-tablecloth establishment. An all-night casino party afterward put on by the Lions or the Rotary. Breakfast in the school cafeteria. A little hanky-panky worked into lulls in the scheduled action. Memories, they say, to last a lifetime. Prom night, USA.

WHERE DO PROMS COME FROM?>

Yearbooks don't start covering proms until the 1930s and 1940s, although an entry in the diary of an Amherst boy records an invitation to one at Smith College in 1894. Perhaps those first proms were really just ordinary junior or senior class dances, with a fancy continental name. The genteel afternoon tea dance, also promoted by colleges for young ladies, is the direct descendant of the once-upon-a-time debutante tea. *Prom* is short for *promenade*, the Grand March, the ceremonial beginning of some colossally important social occasion, a formal nighttime ball, perhaps. A debutante ball! Just as the debutante cotillion stands for the social maturity of the young woman in white, so the prom

Minnesota promgoers, 1955. Minnesota Historical Society

once was—and sometimes still is—the first adult social event in the lives of high schoolers.

For boys and girls alike, it is a coming-out or coming-of-age ceremony, just as formalized and ritualistic as any snooty Christmas cotillion at the Waldorf. The first real dress-up affair. The first use of the family car after dark. A picture-taking event, like a first Communion or a wedding. In an earlier day, the senior prom was the place where the "Best Couple" in the class announced their engagement, right after the crowning of the prom queen and her consort. Prom royalty summons up images of the Veiled Prophet queen and her court, all the various beauty queens on their parade floats, and the fifteen-year-old Latina princesses in their crowns, surrounded by fourteen girlfriends and their dates dressed up as if they were bound for a prom. Queens. Kings. Princesses. Ladies in waiting. Chamberlains. Assorted pages and majordomos. The threshold to adulthood in America seems to run straight through the court of Queen Victoria in her prime.

Or Cinderella in the Disney version, with a brand-new dress, see-through high heels, a prince, and a coronation coach conjured up by magic from a humble pumpkin. A May 2003 news report on a Minneapolis TV station concerned an "outstate" boy who, after two years of dreaming about it, drove his date to their prom aboard the family's new red tractor. She was charmed. Rather than matching her dress to his suit, she wore red, in the exact shade of the tractor. They were the hit of the evening, even though their vehicle hogged five spaces in the high school parking lot. In a recent spring story line, the *Rex Morgan* comic strip had its lovely ingenue arrive at her prom in the basket of a hot-air balloon piloted by the class nerd. Proms are magic nights when Beauty and Beast bond for the sake of the flashiest entrance to the ball.

The prom worked its way down from the college to the high school by gradual increments: a tea dance in one's Sunday best in the early 1900s, a class banquet with dancing and party clothes in the 1920s and 1930s, and proms proper in the 1940s. During the affluent 1950s, proms became more and more formal—that is, expensive and elaborate—thanks in part to the media coverage of debutantes and their doings. In urban and suburban schools, the gym was good enough for sophomores, but the upperclassmen took their proms to country clubs and hotel ballrooms. Competition blossomed. Who had the best dress? The best mode of transportation? The cutest date? The splashiest after-prom party? Today, teenagers with credit cards, cars of their own, and a taste for the good life have made the prom into a pinnacle social event, a dress rehearsal for the mega-wedding, which has also reached surreal heights of elaboration. Schools and parents are no longer the responsible parties, in many cases. The prom has become Prom, a time, a place, a look, a fantasy that requires a capital letter and a wad of cash. Prom is a his-'n'-hers debut without the watchful intervention of doting daddies and nervous moms. The buds and sprigs have taken over the greenhouse and will blossom when and where and how they choose. Prom-zillas, the true fanatics who plot every detail as if their dance were a shuttle mission to Mars, come in both genders, and several combinations thereof.

While debutante rites are exclusive, however, Prom is, or is meant to be, inclusive. Wallis Simpson, the future Duchess of Windsor, bowed to society at the closely guarded Bachelors' Cotillon (the spelling was an affectation!) in 1914, after a dress rehearsal at the choosy Princeton Prom. But the modern-day high school prom is for anybody who wants to come and can cough up the money for a ticket. A date is no longer required, either, if the movies are to be believed. In *Romy and Michele's High School Reunion* (1995) the heroines return to Sagebrush High to improve upon their memories of a dismal senior prom, which the two ditzy friends had attended as each other's dates, in the absence of boys attuned to their gawky charm. Nor does anyone dance with the girls. "At least you looked fantastic, and that's the important thing," says one Madonna wanna-be to the other, in an extended flashback to the worst evening of their lives. Lisa Kudrow, the star of the film, later told *People* magazine that her own prom had been a disaster. "I got my dress on the day of the prom, and it was just awful. I called up my date and canceled."

For every boy consigned to the stag line by a hysterical girlfriend, however, there are ten girls never asked to the prom by some shy, or merely inept, adolescent Lothario. Contemporary advice books directed at prom-bound girls realize that finding a date for the big night can be agony for kids who march to a different drummer. Boys seem to have more options: blowing off the dance and drinking beer instead is a popular choice. But tradition still dictates that a he ask a she, and if he doesn't, the experts say, fly solo. "It isn't the end of the world," according to a recent manual of promming. "It isn't even the end of the prom.

Promgoers stop for a group picture: from left to right, Carl, Danielle, Austin, Caitlin, Derek, and Brigid. Colleen Sheehy

These days, lots of kids go dateless." Or in groups. Or with "pals," to whom no romantic illusions pertain. If all else fails, she can do the asking. "I wasn't invited to the prom," writes comedian Joan Rivers. "I invited the guy and I had to buy my own orchid. . . . Carrie had a better time at her prom than I did."

CARRIE'S AWFUL PROM AND OTHER MOVIE HORRORS

Carrie is Carrie White, the telekinetic central figure in Stephen King's wildly popular 1974 novel. In a recent preface to a new edition of his book, King confides that his homicidal prom queen and her mother, a religious fanatic, were inspired by people he met in his own youth. What is remarkable about *Carrie*, however, is the psychological penetration of the doubts and longings of a young girl who has no expectation of ever being asked to the prom. Through the malice of her classmates, she is invited by a big man on campus, battles her mother for the right to wear an evening gown, and is elected prom queen. And then, in her shining hour, is drenched in a shower of pig blood, much to the amusement of the onlookers. The classic 1976 movie version stars the young Sissy Spacek as a bewildered, tortured Carrie who awakens her powers to burn down the school and her teenage tormenters, and most of the town as well, in one supreme moment of revenge.

Yet before that climactic flash of terror, King captures something of the wonder of arriving at a familiar place only to find it utterly transformed, along with its denizens. "The first thing that struck Carrie when they walked in was Glamor. Not glamor but Glamor. Beautiful shadows rustled about in chiffon, lace, satin, silk. The air was redolent with the odor of flowers. . . . Girls in dresses with low backs, with scooped bodices showing actual cleavage, with Empire waists. Long skirts, pumps. Blinding white dinner jackets, cummerbunds. . . . She knew with suddenness and ease that this moment would be with her always, within hand's reach of memory." Prom dresses and boutonnieres—and Carrie's precious prom favors—are not simply symbols or relics or semiotic texts. They are agents of transformation, tools of the adult world now wielded by a rising generation. Even for girls who come by their prom dates under dubious circumstances, grown-up fashions are the levers and the push buttons of adult society, in which perfumed women in low-cut gowns wield a power often denied them in other circumstances. Carrie White's red, crushed-velvet prom dress (pink satin in the movie) gives new meaning to the term "drop-dead gorgeous."

This encapsulated night of growing up is almost always represented by Hollywood's former promgoers as spectacularly traumatic. *Prom Night* (1980) and its sequels embroider on the *Carrie* theme: during the crowning of the king and queen, a deranged killer attacks the members of the court, in revenge for a long-ago act of meanness. Other films about terrible prom nights seize on class differences and rigid social stratification as obstacles in the path of wretched, prom-bound teens. In *Grease* (1978), John Travolta (previously incinerated in *Carrie*) and Olivia Newton-John are bedeviled on the way to the prom by their reputations; she's one of the "good" girls, while he is a classic greaser from the wrong side of the tracks. *Pretty in Pink* (1986) reverses the situation. She (Molly Ringwald) is the poor girl with the after-school job and the homemade prom dress, while he is a rich boy from the country-club set. Terminal awkwardness, when combined with raging hormones, is another prom hazard. Ben Stiller, wearing a disgusting blue ruffled tux, sets off for the prom with Cameron Diaz, only to run afoul of a balky zipper in his rented trousers. *There's Something about Mary* (1998) then fast-forwards to a future in which poor Ben still pines for the girl of his dreams, his love life permanently stalled at the prom. The raunchy *American Pie* (2000) traces the efforts of four high school buddies sworn to lose their virginity before the end of prom night.

SEX ON PROM NIGHT

To "do it" or not to "do it" that evening seems to be a real enough dilemma. "Dear Abby" has wrestled with the problem of prom-night intimacy every spring for decades: her current successor states flatly that "to lose your virginity to celebrate prom night is not a mature decision." Prom, on the other hand, is all about maturity and tradition, say the guidance counselors and the decorators and the members of the punch-and-cookies committee. "It's a tradition," declared a recent Ohio prom defender. "That's what you look forward to when you get to high school: 'Oh, I get to go to the prom!'" "It's the last event of your senior year, the most fulfilling and memorable moment. . . . It's a beginning of one thing and the closure of another," adds an enthusiastic classmate. A 1976 grad who didn't attend her prom because she didn't have a date told *Seventeen* that she felt like a failure: "Going to the senior prom was the ultimate test. It meant you were ready for adulthood, college, the world. . . . Anyone who hasn't gone to high school in a vacuum knows that getting a diploma isn't nearly as important as that corsage." Plus, added another reader, "You're supposed to fall madly in love, have the best evening of your life, and come away with permanent stars in your eyes." But until the 1990s, when romance became sex and love became a matter of hygiene, most mass-market teen magazines concentrated on makeup, dresses, and strategies for turning the freckle-faced boy next door into a suave prom date. Sex and/or unpleasantness of any sort were strictly taboo.

Suddenly, overnight, circa 1991, the pages of *Seventeen* began to offer timid advice on how to survive the hypothetical prom from hell. What's a girl to do when her date gets drunk and barfs all over her dress? Should you take that tab of acid? If he is determined to have sex, how do you fend him off? (Don't say that you're having your period, counsels a professor of adolescent psychology. Just say no!) As early as 1952, the parents of promgoers were consumed with worry about all of the above—and more. In the Milwaukee area, a local manufacturing concern garnered national publicity by staging a wholesome after-prom affair in a corner of its plant, with the object of keeping teens safely out of motel rooms and bars and off the highways. The concept quickly spread to Indiana, Washington, Missouri, West Virginia, and Arkansas: by the end of the decade, post-proms had become the norm. *Parents' Magazine*, in 1954, surveyed the new cloistered parties under the title "High School Proms without Consequences," the perfect antidote to a "wild, all-night teen-age spree." The attempted reassertion of adult control, however justified by the annual tally of smashups, overdoses, and teen pregnancies, points up an important way in which the prom tradition differs from coming out. The latter is a parental institution, at which a daughter is presented to a carefully screened crop of potential suitors. Although lapses in decorum have been ballyhooed by the press, and debs have taken a more active role in planning their own big night, the rules are set by adult society. Yet, despite the intervention of PTAs and principals, the prom is a teen institution, veiled in the mysteries of peer pressure and steeped in changing mores. If the deb ball looks back to an earlier era of grace and decorum, the prom anticipates the perils and pleasures of adulthood, including sex, alcohol, speed, and difficult choices. And greasers, geeks, freaks, and weirdos are always welcome under the canopy of crepe-paper streamers.

Much of the recent awareness of proms has come to focus on sex. Whether comedic or horrific, the movie prom is always a sexual watershed: an awakening, a parting, a commitment, a final high school frustration. (In fact, watching prom flicks is a favorite pre- or post-prom diversion.) Meanwhile, headlines proclaim the sordid fate of the newborn strangled and left to die in a trash can during a New Jersey prom in June 1997. The new mother, according to friends, had spent the previous week at the mall shopping for prom dresses, seemingly without a care in the world. Asked how high-end proms have changed in recent years, a panel of party planners summed up the expectations of the 1990s prom queen this way: "Versace dress, stretch Humvee, condom." Clothes. Limos. Sex.

THEMES, DECORATIONS, OUTFITS

There is one major prom necessity missing from their list, however. Even when the venue changes from the school gymnasium to the Holiday Inn's Crystal Conference Suite, a proper prom needs a theme. As early as 1939, high school art teachers were pressing their students into service to swaddle prom sites in mirrored balls, wads of cotton, papier-mâché masks, giant figures in silhouette, make-believe towns, and false ceilings made out of cheesecloth. In 1951, song titles were in vogue: "That Old Black Magic" (candlelight, black witch hats), "Stardust" (cardboard stars covered in silver tinfoil; glitter everywhere), and "Deep Purple" (self-explanatory). More demanding were topics such as Old Mexico, South American Cruise, the Gay Nineties, and the Gold Rush, which called for lots of props, big drawings mounted on the walls, and the construction of cardboard scenery.

Farm Journal instructed country kids in the intricacies of creating Candy Land, an Underwater Wonderland, a Japanese Garden, and a Futureworld full of homemade flying saucers. During the 1950s and 1960s, that magazine ran annual contests for the best themes and execution. Willa Blesie, from Minnesota, won an honorable mention in 1966 for her "Mardi-Gras Prom," a simple matter of putting colored plastic bowls of popcorn here and there, with a balloon on a stick in each one; hanging a crown from the ceiling; and giving every promgoer an eye mask and a bag of confetti. A "class artist" of an earlier day, in a memoir published in 1977, describes his run-in with a perky committee-girl, a true prom visionary. "I've got it all pictured in my mind," she confides. "It's gonna be Winter Wonderland this time, right? So what we'll do is build a whole town. Kind of an Alpine town. . . . [W]e can rent some stars and hang them from the ceiling and they'll just twinkle in the light and it'll be so exciting." She, of course, soon disappears, leaving the worker bees with a box of construction paper, thirty feet of streamers, two rolls of aluminum foil, and a box of crayons.

The precocious columnist Joyce Maynard, as a Yale freshman in 1972, looked back on her senior year, when she was cochair of the Oyster River High School prom. She was one of those visionaries—a revolutionary who wanted to do away with tuxes, the queen, and the Grand March. Maynard soon learned, to her great surprise, that proms are about *not* changing things too much. The successful prom chair will drag out the streamers again, pick a song, and get going. But she was curious to see if anything had changed on the high school scene now that President Nixon had announced the mining of Haiphong Harbor. Yale was in an uproar over Vietnam. So was Cheshire High, where the prom theme was "Color My World" and the decorations consisted of chicken-wire palm trees, a tipsy Eiffel Tower, and a set of crepe-paper canopies in the process of being taken down by a much-despised fire marshal. The issue du jour at the high school, however, was streamers. Debbie wanted them: "But proms always have streamers!" The boy who had supplied the silvery weather balloon/world dangling precariously from the rafters thought they spoiled the reflections. The streamers eventually came down, after a heated debate. At Cheshire, the decorations were a big deal. The class didn't want to spend their money on renting a country club: "The whole point is to turn what you've got into something beautiful—like Cinderella," said one of the team. Today, the gym. Tonight, a little bit of paradise. Fancy, shiny, lacy, glittery stuff makes for a beautiful, special, never-to-be-forgotten prom.

The fanciest items at the prom are the dresses. Teen literature wisely devotes most of its energies to that topic. Special springtime-only magazines with titles like *TeenPROM* and *Prom Guide* hit the newsstands, while established journals present special April and May issues. The contents of these publications are instructive: a page or two of routine advice on finding a date and an eye-popping chariot for the evening, and prom-night horror stories from readers and Hollywood idols (movie star Reese Witherspoon, for example, was stood up and went to the prom with her father)—all hidden away amid a flurry of ads for formals, accessories, and beauty products. Boys, when included in photos of young divas at all, are props, the human equivalent of potted palms. The spotlight falls squarely on teenage glamor girls. Girls in deb-style ball gowns, albeit in electric pinks and blues. In slinky numbers. Bare midriffs. Short dresses. Strapless ones. Spangled. Passionate reds. Mys-

Brigid Murphy and Derek Maanum, off to their May 2003 prom in a vintage 1949 Cadillac. Colleen Sheehy

terious blacks. Slit skirts. Peek-a-boo cutouts in strategic spots. Longish Jennifer Aniston hair. Very long JLo locks. The many bed-head looks of Britney Spears. Prom outfits put together from these sources—or any number of Internet prom sites—aim to turn high school girls into the celebrities they admire, to make them into worldly-wise sophisticates

Debutante Sportswear Department, the Higbee Company, Cleveland, Ohio, 1961.
Younger teens were called "sub-debs."

steeped in the secrets of beauty culture. How to maximize (or minimize) bust, hips, shoulders. How to coordinate gown with bag, jewelry, and footwear—and sometimes, almost as an afterthought, his tux.

Anyone who has ever braved the prom boutique (formerly, the Deb Shop) at the local department store during the run-up to the big day cannot fail to be amused and touched by the clots of young women posing for one another in raptures of excitement, with sneakers and jeans peeking out from under the hems of their little lamé numbers. Downstairs, in Special Occasion Shoes, feet that have stood flat on the floor for seventeen years struggle to totter about in four-inch heels. Over in Costume Jewelry, one young fashion maven chides another for even thinking about wearing a gold-tone bracelet with a silver necklace. In Scarves and Handbags, an argument rages on the merits of boas versus stoles. If tradition is one crucial part of the prom equation, the other is innovation. The latest styles. The most grown-up look. The girl transformed into a woman not because her parents say so but because she has remade herself, from head to toe, like Cinderella, bound for the ball, without the intervention of any fairy godmother.

THE PROM NOVEL

A popular novel for teens, much praised for the author's grasp of high school sociometrics, is called *Girl Gives Birth to Own Prom Date* (1996). In Todd Strasser's story, Nicole nudges her grungy next-door neighbor into the ranks of the popular, just in time to take him to the prom. In other words, she constructs a perfect prom for herself, from dress to corsage to remodeled boyfriend. Despite some bumps along the way, the book is about female control, empowerment, and a growing awareness that some things are relatively easy to change while others are not. A cynic might protest that hairdos and plots to manipulate others are hardly ideal lessons for women in training. But the awareness of self, the ability to enjoy and alter the manner in which the self is presented, and the knowledge that the exercise of power does not always yield the hoped-for results are all reasonable guideposts to maturity.

The closing pages of *Girl Gives Birth to Own Prom Date* belong to the date, who finds himself alone on the runway during the Promenade or Grand March feeling quite "okay" as the onlookers cheer his outfit and his special attitude while wearing it. For young men as well as young women, the autoerotic aspects of promgoing are never far from the surface: How terrific I look in this slinky dress! In this cool top hat! How great it all *feels*! Just as the gym becomes a self-created fantasyland, the body becomes something new and unfamiliar, the physical transformations of adolescence given symbolic representation by strange new clothes. So it is that writers on proms find it almost impossible to avoid references to Cinderella, who goes from servant girl to princess in the course of a single glorious evening. In the twenty-first-century version of the tale, the prince, too, will turn out to have been a stable boy—or a high school senior with a sprinkling of acne.

The last word in prom sophistication: Rachel Marling and her prom date, St. Louis,
2000. Stephen and Joan Marling

A popular teen movie of 2003, *What a Girl Wants*, billed as "a Cinderella story for the twenty-first century," does precisely that. A loose remake of *The Reluctant Debutante*, the film acknowledges teenage unfamiliarity with debs by turning the ball into a prom with a slightly more than average quotient of parents standing by. In other words, it celebrates the declension of the aristocratic former into the democratic latter in the person of Amanda Bynes, who grins her merry way through London society armed with an absolute certainty that class divisions are silly and that her new, untitled boyfriend is every inch as good as a duke. The audience, of course, knows she's right: he's an incipient rock star, the contemporary counterpart to royalty. As Amanda arrives at the dance, the camera contrives to sprinkle her with sparkling fairy dust, as a mark of her Cinderella makeover from bumptious kid to dazzling young lady. When the boyfriend finally arrives on the scene, the screen fairly explodes in glitter. It's magic! Two mall rats have turned into his-'n'-hers Cinderellas, without a wand or a fairy godmother in sight! *Girl Gives Birth to Own Prom Date,* and vice versa.

Though his ear for the teen vernacular of angst is finely tuned, Strasser's novel brims with the kinds of ethical insights a parent might attempt to slip into discussions of a much-too-lowcut prom dress. But the majority of the many "novels for young adults" devoted to prom dilemmas situate themselves squarely in teen or preteen culture, celebrating dress mania, date hysteria, and the debate over whether to "go all the way" with the earnestness of a sophomore peering into the gym during the last-minute frenzy of streamer-hanging for the senior prom. The twin girls in the prom volume of Francine Pascal's *Sweet Valley High* series (1998) pore over *Dazzle* magazine for hairstyle tips, rejecting the big dos beloved of Miss America candidates. Surrounded by a gaggle of girlfriends, they try on slinky, sexy sheaths studded with rhinestones and stand back in awe at the results: "It made Jessica look like a confident, fully grown *woman* instead of the sixteen-year-old she was." And Jessica, posing in the mirror, twirling this way and that for best effect, agrees. She's beautiful. "It's *perfection.*" William McCants's *Much Ado about Prom Night* (1995) also trots out the familiar prom motifs: the boy who plans to rent a chauffeured hearse for the big night and the girl who finds a "pretty white-and-silver dress with a tulle skirt" and all the accessories—and then dyes her hair an unfortunate pumpkin orange by

Beth Marling and her prom date, St. Louis, 1998. Stephen and Joan Marling

mistake. You can take the fairy godmother out of the prom story, apparently, but Disney's pumpkin coach lingers on in memory.

Even "Sabrina, the Teenage Witch" materializes on the prom scene in a 1999 novel based on the TV series of the same name, helping to conjure up a Camelot theme with paper dragons and a cardboard castle where the photographer sets up shop. But a surprising number of prom books pick up where Stephen King left off, using cardboard backdrops as scenes for murder, mayhem, and terror. R. L. Stine, the dean of scary stories for teens, uncorks a scenario in which five prom queen candidates are killed off, one after another. The usual paraphernalia—the gardenia corsage, the sexy black dress—fleshes out a story that suggests just how traumatic prom preparations can be for the average student, even if she is not *The Prom Queen* (1992) slashed to death on the eve of her coronation. Where proms are concerned, Stine knows, some things are much worse than death. *Prom Night* (1999), an anthology of short stories, includes bug-eyed sci-fi monsters in prom dresses, a boy who wants to go to the prom with a dead girl, Satanists casting spells on potential dates, and worse. Both the authors and the teens they describe repeat the same prom night mantra of semi-facts: that the prom movies are all true, that proms are the stepchildren of fancy society debuts, and that this will be a night of earthshaking change, a true rite of passage, the more excessive the better. A Bacchanalia. A night to remember. Heaven on Earth (a great prom theme!). A horror show. Dylan Klebold and Eric Harris, who attended the Columbine High School prom on April 17, 1999, came back to school several days later, as prom gossip still echoed in the halls, and slaughtered thirteen people before turning the guns on themselves. A night to remember in Colorado.

But the prom goes on. And given the ubiquity of promming—in parts of the Midwest, it is impossible to rent a limo in April or May—why don't today's etiquette manuals have much to say about it? Even books that still lay down the law concerning the minutiae of debuts treat the prom as an afterthought. Marjabelle Young Stewart, author of *The New Etiquette: Real Manners for Real People* (1997), limits her prom wisdom to commonsense generalities. Proms are expensive. The one who issues the invitation buys the tickets. The young man buys the flowers. Stand up straight. And "whatever you do, don't let the mood of the evening get away from you. This is a big night in your life, and it should be treated as such." Of the experts, only "Miss Manners" gets to the heart of the matter. This is a teen event, she insists, and teens can figure it out for themselves—except, perhaps, for how the rough equality between the sexes can be skewed by prom clothes. She tells the girls not to be alarmed if he holds her wrap or opens the door for her: "These are merely little superficial social customs, graced by tradition and pleasant to practice. They go with your pretty dress, which also, you may notice, bears a significant gender distinction from your young man's formal clothing, and are not to be overanalyzed for sociological content." Go with the flow. There may even be kissing involved.

Miss Manners's mantle of cast-iron gentility prevents her from entertaining the notion of rampant teenage sexual activity or acknowledging the infamous case of Melissa Drexler, who gave birth to a six-pound baby boy in a rest-room stall during her 1997 senior prom—and then returned to dance the night away with the father of the child. Yet there is a sense in which proms aim to control teenage sexuality by encouraging high school kids to wear highly gendered adult costumes while attending a ritual event closely supervised by PTAs and school boards. The flowers, the pictures, and the outfits make the prom into a mock wedding, minus the honeymoon; that was clearly the intent in the 1940s and 1950s, when chaperonage was more intrusive and deb shops were stocked with pouffy white gowns that imitated bridal attire. The clothes and the awkwardness with which they were worn bespoke an innocence that most high school seniors of the twenty-first century would take pains to deny.

TRUE PROM DISASTERS

But sexuality crops up to bedevil prom planners even in supposedly enlightened eras, like the heyday of Led Zeppelin. In 1980, a community crisis erupted in Elmore City, Oklahoma, a small town with a mid-nineteenth-century law against public dancing. That winter, students at the local high school petitioned the principal for the right to have a prom, and debate over the request splintered the town of 653. The pastor of the Pentecostal church (and father of two teenage daughters) spoke for the antis. "When boys and girls hold each other, they get sexually aroused," he thundered. "You can believe what you want, but one thing leads to another." At a town meeting, an indignant citizen predicted a surge in pregnancies at the school in the months after the dance "because when boys and girls breathe in each other's ears, that's the next step." After much bitter wrangling, however, the prom went on: "Stairway to Heaven," it was called, in a backhanded tribute to the theological opposition. The school cafeteria, where the ear-breathing finally commenced, was decorated with silver stars on a blue paper background, an aluminum foil moon, and a sequined cardboard stairway.

That was also the year in which Aaron Fricke took Paul Guilbert to the Cumberland, Rhode Island, senior prom, thanks to a ruling from the U.S. District Court, supported by the Rhode Island Gay Liberation Task Force. Guilbert, who had graduated the year before, had been denied permission to attend his own prom with a boy, and because his parents had refused to file suit on behalf of their minor child, the case never went to court. So he came back and tried again with the help of eighteen-year-old Fricke, who did have standing under the law. The pair turned up in contrasting tuxedos and danced the night away, under the protection of Task Force officials. But when Aaron rested his head on Paul's shoulder during a slow dance, the other promgoers ringed the couple and stared in horrified fascination. Some left the dance, resentful that their night had been tainted by the uproar. "They wanted it to be *their* prom," said a sympathetic superintendent of schools. In the aftermath of the much-publicized event, Fricke's parents separated and Guilbert's threw him out. The dance at Cumberland High was not one of the corsage-and-paper-moon confections that *Life* still dropped in on from time to time.

Aaron and Paul were soon followed by Marie and Stephanie of Salinas, California, who went to court because their high school would not allow either one of them to go dateless, or "stag," to the prom. So Marie Hawkins, in a tux, took best friend Stephanie Salgado, in a flowered prom dress. They both had a great time but shied away from branding their lawsuit as a homosexual issue, although Marie's home was sprayed with antigay graffiti. Instead, they cited feminist principles: "We don't need to be on the arm of a male to go to the prom or do anything," said Ms. Hawkins. "We can do it ourselves." In a survey of the season's proms published in the *New Yorker* in 1981, a group of seniors from Queens said much the same thing. They didn't necessarily want to spend prom night in a clutch of girls, but, as one independent young woman (who bought her own corsage) put it, "I don't want to be obligated to a guy—that's not what I want." It was important to dress up and go, but on one's own terms.

In the past decade, even openly gay couples seem to have worked their way into the loosening structure of proms without the usual hullabaloo. In 1992, *Glamour* followed the prom preparations of Heidi Leiter and Missy Peters as a gay pride fashion statement. Although some classmates were shocked to learn that one or another of the girls was a lesbian ("Oh, gross. It makes me want to puke!" cried one politically incorrect young lady), nobody at Virginia's Osbourn High seemed too upset about the prospect of two girls in tuxes (and high heels) on the dance floor. As for Missy and Heidi, they selected black cutaways with tails and high heels to avoid role-playing as "boy" and "girl." And both wore lavender cummerbunds, of course.

It seems just as typical of the times that a sophomore honor student from West Palm Beach, Florida, should have taken her prom date to court when he didn't show up as expected. In an 1989 lawsuit, she listed her preprom expenses: new shoes, a hairdo, a sprig of baby's breath for said hairdo, and court costs, or a total of $81.28. The $280 prom dress she had been able to return for a full refund. The errant date claimed to have broken his ankle, but neither she nor the judge deemed the excuse sufficient for skipping the prom. The jilted promgoer got her money in full.

And then there is the story of the chubby kid from Waukesha, Wisconsin, who couldn't stop asking girls to the prom. Twenty-five ladies took him up on his offer. By the time May 1991 rolled around, however, only twelve were still left—and that was a mercy, since Bill Johnston had begun to realize that his mega-date could cost as much as $500, counting dinners, tickets, flowers, tux, and incidentals. It was then that he decided to talk his way into free food, limos, and all the rest, leaving him with a bill for $62.50, most of that for tips. A pretty average guy until prom night, Bill became an instant celebrity and went home starry-eyed, with a serious crush on a member of his entourage. But since he had spent so much time on the logistics for prom night, he missed graduation by a course or two and had to spend the summer back in high school. One wonders whether that entitled Bill to another crack at the senior prom next year.

Bill is a rare exception to the rule that prom night is a "chicks' night." That girls run the show. After all, they played with Barbie dolls that came dressed in prom outfits and Ken was, in the end, no more than a plastic accessory. Boys know that girls will cancel at the drop of a feather boa if a better date looms into view. That tuxes cost a fortune—and who wants to wear a badly fitting suit that forty other guys have suffered in before? That something major will go wrong. That no female on earth has saved her virginity just for him on this special night. That, contrary to myth, all teenagers do not discover true love at the prom, either. Prom is a fairy tale, like Santa Claus, a pretty lie high schoolers have been duped into believing, generation after generation. Acne will blossom like gardenias hours before the prom. The suit will smell bad. Punch will spill. Your date will spend two hours weeping in the rest room. Your friends will act like morons. The theme will be dumb. "Prom blows chunks," as an inelegant young critic of the custom put it in a recent Internet rave. It is *not* "the most blessed event that has even taken place in the history of mankind." Only girls believe that bull_ _ _ _!

A skeptical teenage boy asked to discuss Prom in the pages of *Newsweek* labeled the whole ritual a snare and a delusion, the big "American fairy tale" that turns out to be "a Simpsons' rendition of the Cinderella ball." He was right: the prom is all about fantasy. Just as magazines run their annual features on celebrity promgoing, so every spring prom-bound teens dress up like stars and strut their stuff as though they were film idols promenading down the red carpet on Oscar night. But at the same time, the high school prom is a barometer of real social attitudes that spill over from the adult world into the lives of their children. The 1990s witnessed the first all gay and lesbian alternative prom in Los Angeles. In Paducah, Kentucky, a senior paralyzed in a school shooting attended her prom in a wheelchair, reminding her classmates of the realities of life in a gun culture. A high school principal in Wedowee, Alabama, tried to cancel the prom because it was rumored that interracial couples were going to attend; in the wake of the resulting controversy, someone burned down the school. In Dedham, Massachusetts, another principal refused to allow one girl to bring another to the junior prom unless they could prove they were a gay couple. A disastrous flood in Grand Forks, North Dakota, threatened to cancel the prom, until a San Francisco dress designer shipped three hundred fifty prom

"After the Ball" Barbie, the ultimate deb: first a fashion doll, c. 1966—now a fashion plate.

outfits to a local aircraft hangar still above water. There, as fire and flood waters rampaged through town, the prom went on as usual. In a Florida school district near Orlando, a six-foot-tall gay male was told that he'd be barred from the prom if he showed up in drag, in a full-length red gown with spaghetti straps and rhinestone accessories. But he went anyway, after a flood of adverse publicity silenced the principal (who still insisted, however, that this was a one-time exemption from the unstated rules of promming).

Why are proms such an enduring tradition that whole industries would fail if teenagers ignored all the prom movies—with their helpful suggestions on dress, decor, decorum, and mayhem—and held tree-plantings or 10K runs instead? Are proms about spring? Closure? Endings? New beginnings? Being grown up? Queen for a day? Cinderella? Buying all kinds of new stuff? Making memories and "Kodak Moments"? A wrist corsage, saved for months in the refrigerator, right next to the celery? An evening of make-believe that holds the bigger problems of life at bay: Evening in Paris? Stairway to Heaven? Mood Indigo? Or is it coming out, with the assurance that the next morning you can creep back in for a little while longer? A debutante ball held beneath a glittering moon made out of aluminum foil, cardboard, and hope!

After the Ball

Holding a debut is generally regarded as an affectation of the very rich—or a smug admission that one is rich. In an interview with the *Ladies' Home Journal* in 1960, singer–movie star–orange juice magnate Bing Crosby said that he'd probably have a coming-out party for his baby daughter someday. "I've never been against things like that as long as the parents could afford them," he crooned. "Debuts are like honeymoons. A girl may look ahead to hers for only a few years, but she'll look back on it forever." Like the prom or the bat mitzvah or the presentation of Laredo, Texas, girls in gowns so big and heavy that the buds must arrive at the ball strapped upright into tractor-trailers, the debut makes for vivid memories. It stops the regular pulse of time so dramatically, so decisively, that it cannot be forgotten.

But, despite the endorsement of a much-loved star, the association with excessive wealth and rancid eccentricity never goes away. In the 1930s, the era of the grossly expensive debut and the canonically silly debutante, the costs reinforced the yawning gap between rich and poor. The rich really *were* different from you and me, a breed apart in their willingness to court publicity for spending money on fripperies while a third of the nation suffered through the depression in poverty. Class: odd behavior, affected manners, entitlement, and general snootiness on the part of the deb class made cotillions an irresistible target for the press.

Debutantes and their parents used to be as exotic to readers as two-headed calves and cannibals—freaks of nature or culture, but well worth watching, if only for amusement. In short, celebrities. Hollywood grasped the entertainment value of the "society dame" and her flighty daughter even before the movies began to talk: in 1922, Rudolph Valentino attended a cotillion and a debutante tea in the course of one steamy feature film. The Marx Brothers made a career out of making merciless fun of rich ladies with airs and lots of diamonds. Why, even Judy Garland made a stab at playing a deb (although a very nice one, indeed).

And what, exactly, was that white tulle dress business all about? Unsullied innocence? Virginity? Fragility? Frigidity? A wedding yet to come? In a recent paperback thriller, a hard-boiled detective describes the case against a "perp" as foolproof. "This thing's wrapped tighter than a deb with new tits," says the cop. "It's that bad?" asks his female sidekick. Very bad. Debs are snooty and snotty and uptight, which is surely part of their allure in ads for escort services that feature cool lasses in white gowns coyly adjusting their garter belts. These ladies of the evening are, in the words of one lubricious advertisement, "in a class of their own." The price of a date provides the illusion of ravishing an untouchable—or proving that the rich aren't really any different from you and me. The same perverse stereotype underlies the music of the White Trash Debutantes, the rock band said to combine the sensibilities of the gutter lowlife with "poor little rich girl soap-opera ingenue ennui." Phew!

Finally, and most obviously, the phrase *coming out* means something a little different in the gay community. In 1997, comic Ellen DeGeneres revealed that she was a lesbian just prior to an episode of her TV sitcom in which the lead character did the same thing. In response, the Gay and Lesbian Alliance against Defamation of Los Angeles prepared kits for holding "Come Out with Ellen" parties from coast to coast. The event was a national fund-raiser, but it was also an opportunity for others to reveal their sexual orientation—to come out of the closet. Similarly, beauty contests for cross-dressing men are also known as cotillions. In the end, both gay and straight debuts are about the same things: self-revelation and a change in one's social status, with a strong sexual component. Yet some leaders of the movement object to party kits and beaded evening gowns. "Consumerism is not a replacement for liberation," remarked a disillusioned activist after the DeGeneres stir had subsided.

Reduced to its lowest common denominator, a debut or a quinceañera or a prom is a coming-of-age ritual for women (and sometimes for men). In other times and places, adulthood was signified by scarification or performance of a difficult task. The American debutante may well be scarred by her experience and the whole ritual fraught with difficulty, but the real similarities come in the oddity of the event, its distinctive aesthetic, its difference from everyday life. Dresses and flowers and flowers and tiaras are all about identifying a new, adult member of a community: country-club America, the jet set, midwesterners, the African-American neighborhoods of Detroit, the college-bound class of 2004 from Anywhere, USA. And so debs of one sort or another dance and smile at the guests and pose for pictures and pour tea.

The tea morphed into a grander affair as a tide of national wealth raised the ships of entrepreneurs and robber barons. And in an age when Horatio Alger proved over and over again that any poor boy could grow up to be a millionaire, the drovers and the seamstresses who stood tiptoe on the sidewalks outside Delmonico's to watch the pretty debs skitter by on their way to glittering balls were justified in thinking, or hoping, that their own daughters might join the dancers someday soon. In the 1920s and 1930s, debs were movie stars who didn't live in Hollywood. They were America's store-window mannequins to which furs and jewelry and fancy cars—along with particular brands of soap, cigarettes, and coffee—were readily attached. They were, depending on one's own situation, symbols of the underlying economic stability of the land or potential targets for kidnappers, protesters, and social critics arguing for a more equitable distribution of the nation's resources. Like Katharine Hepburn and Bette Davis, they were fantastic creatures from mirrored penthouses whose strange accents and peculiar ways provided welcome diversions from life's daily miseries. They were glamorous. Beautiful. And, oh! The clothes!

The new postwar prosperity revived cotillions, proms, and pageantry. The usual suspects groomed their daughters for Waldorf debuts, albeit group events now, under the protective umbrella of charitable fund-raising. In the meantime, however, Americans of every persuasion realized that they could do it themselves. They could buy dresses and hire bands. They could move the prom from the gym to a spanking-new hotel ballroom. Eventually, when the anti-Communist hysteria of the 1950s had run its course, they could honor their children's descent from ancestors who had not arrived on the *Mayflower*. When the civil rights movement had made college accessible to the grandchildren of slaves, they could honor their own achievements and aspirations. And when the Vietnam protests had fallen silent, they could indulge their suburban taste for the good life. At the high school level, teenagers with after-school jobs could run their own proms and play at being Jennifer Aniston and Brad Pitt for a day. Everybody could be a deb, or something just like it! Everywoman could be Cinderella. And every frog (oops! I meant man!) her (or his) Prince Charming.

There are lots of good reasons for having debuts. To beef up the reputation of a cow town. To create an elite that can support schemes for civic betterment. To affirm the value of women. To demonstrate pride in one's family, or a rage for order. Class, celebrity, community. Most of all, though, debbing means having a monumental good time. There must have been many debs, like Eleanor Roosevelt, who felt awkward and out of place at their debuts, but that did not stop Mrs. Roosevelt from holding one in honor of her niece. A debut was a learning experience, at the very least. At best, well—it was a ball!

Or a ball gown. After everything else has been discussed and dispensed with, the fancy dress remains the fundamental, indispensable attribute of the debutante. Often white—but not always (quinceañero dresses come in pink and blue these days). Luscious. Decorative. Unfamiliar. It *feels* different. It rustles. It pinches and prods in all the right places. The sheltered nineteenth-century maiden could not help but notice that she was on display, shoulders and bosom and all. The champagne-guzzling vamp of the 1920s chose her gown with that very idea in mind. The senior bound for the prom aspires to be the picture in the fan magazine. High heels. Special jewelry. Gloves. A wrap. The body becomes—for a moment, at any rate—an alien thing, separate from the self. A work of art. Mind and body part company, in a rustle of tulle. Which one am I? The being that plans and primps and embellishes? Or the beautiful young creature who finally emerges from her curlers, ready to dance? The girl with a picture of a dress hidden in the pages of her diary—or the woman wearing one?

Acknowledgments

My debutantes never would have made it to the ball without the best efforts of my fairy godmother–like research assistants. One of them was actually a fairy godfather. David Slater did exhaustive research on the coming-out rituals of the black community in Detroit and their white counterparts. He scoured the library at the Winterthur Museum for rare etiquette texts that could not be found in the Midwest. He also worked with me in Kansas City during a particularly hot summer to turn up documentation on the Jewel Ball. And, as if all that weren't enough, he put himself in charge of obtaining photographs for the book, while completing two graduate degrees. I owe him a great debt of gratitude—and showers of cotillion favors—for his help and concern.

Bouquets to Cassie Wilkins, who took time out from her own doctoral studies to comb various San Francisco repositories and to copy relevant periodical articles there and elsewhere. And to Leigh Roethke, eBay expert and student of Hispanic popular culture, who was quick to share information and to act as my on-line purchasing agent.

During another hot summer, my family in St. Louis immersed themselves in Veiled Prophet lore on my behalf; many thanks to my brother Stephen, sister-in-law Joan, and nieces Beth and Rachel for responding to my pitiful cries for help (and prom pictures).

Jessie Hite of Austin, Texas, generously shared her deb scrapbook (including the original bar tab!) with me. The late Libbie Mohr of Atlanta, who knew *everything* about Southern debs, sent snapshots and answered questions. Lisa Fischman, at the Atlanta College of Art, represented my interests in places below the Mason-Dixon line. M. Sue Kendall, without whose perpetual help and interest my writing would be a lonely task indeed, shared amazing deb and prom relics and served as my gowned spy at several Philadelphia debuts. Colleen Sheehy volunteered her daughter's prom photos for the cause.

Nancy Jackson, my editor at the University Press of Kansas, has been patient, enthusiastic, and smart—a true prom queen (her white dress was really for a sorority pledge) in a business suit! Michael Kammen, a prom king of long standing, read the manuscript on short notice and saved me from many errors in good taste and manners.

Finally, in this place, I want to thank my own long-ago prom dates (unnamed here, they will be pleased to note!) for the orchids and the wrist corsages, the fancy dinners, the freshly waxed cars, the gallantry, and the smooching that went on under the bleachers. You never forget a Prince Charming in a fancy suit. And you never forget being Cinderella, powdered, perfumed, and off to the ball.

A Note on Sources

began this book in the Newspaper and Periodicals Collection of the Meredith O. Wilson Library at the University of Minnesota by examining the society pages of the nation's newspapers during the several "seasons" preferred by debutantes during the course of the nineteenth and twentieth centuries. Most of my textural research comes from months of reading descriptions of dresses, flower arrangements, guest lists, and the like in the following papers: *Atlanta Constitution, Baltimore Sun, Boston Transcript, Chicago Daily News, Chicago Tribune, Detroit Free Press, Detroit News, Detroit Saturday Night, Kansas City Independent, Kansas City Journal, Kansas City Star, Kansas City Times, Michigan Chronicle, Minneapolis Star Tribune, Minneapolis Tribune, New Orleans Times-Picayune, New York Herald Tribune, New York Post, New York Times* (and *New York Times Magazine*), *Philadelphia Inquirer, St. Louis Post-Dispatch, St. Paul Pioneer Press,* and *San Francisco Chronicle.*

The Internet has changed standard research methods a great deal, and I was delighted with what searches of *debutante* and *cotillion* called to life in terms of personal reminiscences, inquiries, postings by social organizations, and, above all, ads for books, movies, clothing, and souvenir items. This scattergun assortment of pictures and ideas cannot, however, take the place of a well-organized collection of documents, artifacts, clippings, and photographs. The archives and collections used in preparing this study include the California Historical Society, Cotillion Club Inc. of Detroit, Detroit Public Library, Grosse Pointe Historical Society, Kansas City Public Library, Minneapolis Public Library, Minnesota Historical Society, Missouri Historical Society, San Francisco History Center, San Francisco Public Library, St. Louis Public Library, special collections of the University of Missouri at Kansas City, Children's Literature Collection at the Anderson Library of the University of Minnesota, Winterthur Museum Library, and Wisconsin Center for Film and Theater Research at the Wisconsin Historical Society.

One of the benefits of learning about a subject by rummaging through newspapers, documents, and magazines is that the context in which a given event took place becomes clearer. So it was a pleasure to spend the cotillion and prom seasons with *California Life, Ebony, Harper's Bazaar, Ladies' Home Journal, Life, Look, Newsweek,* the *New Yorker, People Weekly, Printers Ink, Prom,* the *Saturday Evening Post, Seventeen, Time, Town and Country, Vogue, W,* and a variety of other magazines and regional journals that have paid attention to American social life.

For accounts of high society's rites and rituals in New York and elsewhere, the most rewarding studies are Cleveland Amory, *Who Killed Society?* (New York, 1960); Edwin G. Burrows and Mike Wallace, *Gotham: A History of New York City to 1898* (New York, 1999); Allen Churchill, *The Upper Crust* (Englewood Cliffs, N.J., 1970); M. H. Dunlap, *Gilded City* (New York, 2000); Stephen Richard Higley, *Privilege, Power and Place: The Geography of the American Upper Class* (Lanham, Md., 1995); Lucy Kavaler, *The Private World of High Society* (New York, 1960); Maureen E. Montgomery, *Displaying Women: Spectacles of Leisure in Edith Wharton's New York* (New York, 1998); Lloyd R. Morris, *Incredible New York: High Life and Low Life of the Last Hundred Years* (New York, 1951); Kate Simon, *Fifth Avenue: A Very Social History* (New York, 1978); and Dixon Wecter, *The Saga of American Society: A Record of Social Aspiration, 1607–1937* (New York, 1969).

Also useful are Lois Banner, *American Beauty* (New York, 1983); Martha Banta, *Imaging American Women* (New York, 1987); Sven Beckert, *The Monied Metropolis: New York City and the Consolidation of the American Bourgeoisie, 1850–1896* (New York, 2001); David Black, *The King of Fifth Avenue: The Fortunes of August Belmont* (New York, 1981); Paul Bourget, *Outre-mer* (New York, 1895); David Cannadine, *The Decline and Fall of the British Aristocracy* (New York, 1999); Howard Chandler Christy, *The American Girl* (New York, 1906); Michael Denning, *Mechanic Accents: Dime Novels and Working-Class Culture in America* (New York, 1987); G. William Domhoff, *The Higher Circles: The Governing Class in America* (New York, 1971); Erika Doss, ed., *Looking at Life Magazine* (Washington, D.C., 2001); B. Downey Fairfax, *Portrait of an Era, as Drawn by Charles Dana Gibson* (New York, 1936); Debra L. Gimlin, *Body Work* (Berkeley, Calif.,

2002); David C. Hammack, *Power and Society: Greater New York at the Turn of the Century* (New York, 1982); Frederic Cople Jaher, ed., *The Rich, the Well Born, and the Powerful* (Urbana, Ill. 1973); Patricia Johnston, *Real Fantasies: Edward Steichen's Advertising Photographs* (Berkeley, Calif., 1997); Carolyn Kitch, *The Girl on the Magazine Cover* (Chapel Hill, N.C., 2001); James Lever, *Memorable Balls* (London, 1954); Alfred Allan Lewis, *Ladies and Not-So-Gentlewomen* (New York, 2000); Roland Marchand, *Advertising the American Dream: Making Way for Modernity, 1920–1940* (Berkeley, Calif., 1985); Maureen E. Montgomery, *"Gilded Prostitution": Status, Money, and Transatlantic Marriages, 1870–1914* (New York, 1989); M. C. Nathan, *The Pleasure of Your Company: RSVP* (San Francisco, 1968); Ellen M. Plante, *Women at Home in Victorian America* (New York, 1997); Wendy Wick Reaves, *Celebrity Caricature in America* (New Haven, Conn., 1998); Mrs. John King Van Rensselaer, *The Social Ladder* (New York, 1924); Stanley Weintraub, *Edward the Caresser* (New York, 2001); and Helen Worden, *Society Circus* (New York, 1937).

On the playgrounds of the rich and famous: Ralph Blumenthal, *Stork Club* (New York, 2000); Henry Collins Brown, *In the Golden Nineties* (Hastings-on-Hudson, N.Y., 1928); George S. Chappell, *The Restaurants of New York* (New York, 1925); Albert Stevens Crockett, *Peacocks on Parade* (New York, 1931); Lewis A. Erenberg, *Steppin' Out: New York Nightlife and the Transformation of American Culture, 1980–1930* (Westport, Conn., 1981); and Stanley Walker, *The Night Club Era* (New York, 1933).

On courtship and marriage: Beth L. Bailey, *From Front Porch to Back Seat: Courtship in Twentieth-Century America* (Baltimore, 1988); Elizabeth Freeman, *The Wedding Complex: Forms of Belonging in Modern American Culture* (Durham, N.C., 2002); Paul Fussell, *Uniforms* (Boston, 2002); Christopher Hibbert, *Queen Victoria: A Personal History* (New York, 2000); Chrys Ingraham, *White Weddings: Romancing Heterosexuality in Popular Culture* (New York, 1999); Lynn Peril, *Think Pink* (New York, 2002); and Arlene Hamilton Stewart, *A Bride's Book of Wedding Traditions* (New York, 1995).

On regional and national pageantry: Thomas Willing Balch, *The Philadelphia Assemblies* (Philadelphia, 1916); Sarah Banet-Weiser, *The Most Beautiful Girl in the World: Beauty Pageants and National Identity* (Berkeley, Calif., 1999); Richard P. Coleman and Bernice L. Neugarten, *Social Status in the City* (San Francisco, 1971); Frank Deford, *There She Is*

(New York, 1971); Michaele Thurgood Haynes, *Dressing Up Debutantes: Pageantry and Glitz in Texas* (New York, 1998); Samuel Kinser, *Carnival, American Style* (Chicago, 1990); Henri Schindler, *Mardi Gras, New Orleans* (New York, 1997); Thomas Spencer, *The St. Louis Veiled Prophet Celebration: Power on Parade, 1877–1995* (Columbia, Mo., 2000); and Steven M. Stowe, *Intimacy and Power in the Old South: Ritual in the Lives of the Planters* (Baltimore, 1989).

On racial and ethnic coming-of-age rituals: Lawrence Otis Graham, *Our Kind of People: Inside America's Black Upper Class* (New York, 1999); Mary D. Lankford, *Quinceañera: A Latina's Journey to Womanhood* (Brookfield, Conn., 1994); Annette Lynch, *Dress, Gender, and Cultural Change: Asian American and African American Rites of Passage* (New York, 1999); Elizabeth H. Pleck, *Celebrating the Family: Ethnicity, Consumer Culture, and Family Rituals* (Cambridge, Mass., 2000); and Michele Salcedo, *Quinceañera! The Essential Guide to Planning the Perfect Sweet Fifteen Celebration* (New York, 1997).

On famous and infamous debutantes: Carl Sferrazza Anthony, *First Ladies* (New York, 1990); Sydney Biddle Barrows, *The Mayflower Madame* (New York, 1986); Sarah Bradford, *America's Queen: The Life of Jacqueline Kennedy Onassis* (New York, 2000); Mrs. Winthrop Chanler, *Roman Spring* (Boston, 1934); Elsie de Wolfe, *After All* (New York, 1935); Gioia Diliberto, *Debutante: The Story of Brenda Frazier* (New York, 1987); Carol Felsenthal, *Alice Roosevelt Longworth* (New York, 1988); James Fox, *Five Sisters: The Langhornes of Virginia* (New York, 2000); Cornelia Guest et al., *The Debutante's Guide to Life* (New York, 1986); Dean Jennings, *Barbara Hutton: A Candid Biography* (New York, 1968); Kitty Kelley, *Nancy Reagan: The Unauthorized Biography* (New York, 1991); Pamela Clarke Keogh, *jackiestyle* (New York, 2001); Greg King, *The Duchess of Windsor* (New York, 1999); Joseph P. Lash, *Eleanor and Franklin* (New York, 1971); Alice Roosevelt Longworth, *Crowded Hours* (New York, 1933); Donald Spoto, *Jacqueline Bouvier Kennedy Onassis: A Life* (New York, 2000); Edith Wharton, *A Backward Glance* (New York, 1998); John Whitcomb and Claire Whitcomb, *Real Life at the White House* (New York, 2000); Frances M. Wolcott, *Heritage of Years: Kaleidoscopic Memories* (New York, 1932); and Morton D. Zabel, *Ruth Draper: Her Drama and Characters* (New York, 1960).

The most rewarding discussions of making a debut are often found in works of fiction, including Louis Auchincloss, *Manhattan Monologues*

(New York, 2002); Margaret Culkin Banning, *Country Club People* (New York, 1923) and *Out in Society* (New York, 1939); John Berendt, *Midnight in the Garden of Good and Evil* (New York, 1994); Anita Brookner, ed., *The Collected Stories of Edith Wharton* (New York, 1991); Janet Dailey, *Night of the Cotillion*, an e-book (2001); Josephine Dodge Daskam, *Smith College Stories* (New York, 1900); Mrs. E. F. Ellet, *Love in a Maze; or, the Debutante's Disenchantment* (New York, 1865); F. Scott Fitzgerald, *This Side of Paradise* (New York, 1996); Heywood Gould, *One Dead Debutante* (New York, 1975); William Douglas Home, *The Reluctant Debutante: A Play in Two Acts* (New York, 1957); Stephanie Laurens, *A Season for Scandal* (New York, 2001); Clare Boothe Luce, *The Women* (New York, 1937); Mary McCarthy, *The Group* (New York, 1954); Olive Higgins Prouty, *Stella Dallas: A Story of Mother Love* (New York, 1923); Lela Horn Richards, *Blue Bonnet: Debutante* (Boston, 1916); Jane Flaum Singer, *The Debutantes* (New York, 1982); Whitney Terrell, *The Huntsman* (New York, 2001); and Edith Wharton, *New York Novels* (New York, 1998).

The most informative sources are etiquette manuals and other kinds of prescriptive literature on mingling with the "best people." These works also provide a calendar of changes in the various debutante rituals, including teas, receptions, balls, styles of dancing, flowers, and so forth: Letitia Baldrige, *Amy Vanderbilt's Everyday Etiquette* (New York, 1981); Louise Fiske Bryson, *Every-day Etiquette: A Manual of Good Manners* (New York, 1890); Gerald Carson, *The Polite Americans* (New York, 1966); Maud C. Cooke, *20th Century Hand-Book of Etiquette* (Philadelphia, 1899); Francis W. Crowninshield, *Manners for the Metropolis* (New York, 1908); Juliana Cutting, a three-part series of articles on debuts, *Saturday Evening Post* (April, May, and June 1933); Lillian Eichler, *Etiquette Problems in Pictures* (New York, 1922); Mrs. Ellet, *The Queens of American Society* (New York, 1867); Marion Harland and Virginia Van de Water, *Everyday Etiquette: A Practical Manual of Social Usages* (Indianapolis, 1905); Mrs. Burton Harrison, *The Well-Bred Girl in Society* (Philadelphia, 1898); Ardern Holt, *Fancy Dresses Described; or, What to Wear at Fancy Balls* (London, 1884); John F. Kasson, *Rudeness and Civility: Manners in Nineteenth-Century Urban America* (New York, 1990); Helen Carroll Livingstone, *The White House Book of Etiquette* (Chicago, 1903); Abby Buchanan Longstreet, *Social Etiquette of New York* (New York, 1883); S. L. Louis, *Decorum: A Practical Treatise on Etiquette and Dress of the Best American Society* (New

York, 1881); Judith Martin, *Miss Manners' Guide for the Turn-of-the-Millennium* (New York, 1990); Mrs. Sara B. Maxwell, *Manners and Customs of To-Day* (Des Moines, Iowa, 1890); Emily Post, *How to Behave—Though a Debutante* (Garden City, N.J., 1928); Arthur M. Schlesinger, *Learning How to Behave: A Historical Study of Etiquette Books* (New York, 1946); Mary Elizabeth Wilson Sherwood, *The Art of Entertaining* (New York, 1892), *An Epistle to Posterity* (New York, 1897), *Etiquette; the American Code of Manners* (New York, 1884), and *Manners and Social Usages* (New York, 1918); *Social Etiquette of New York* (New York, 1883); Frances Stevens and Frances M. Smith, *Etiquette, Health and Beauty* (New York, 1889); Marjabelle Young Stewart, *The New Etiquette* (New York, 1997); Robert Tomes, *The Bazar Book of Decorum* (New York, 1874); Richard A. Wells, *Manners, Culture and Dress of the Best American Society* (Omaha, Nebr., 1891); Annie R. White, *Polite Society at Home and Abroad* (Chicago, 1891); and [A Woman of Fashion], *Etiquette for Americans* (Chicago, 1898).

On proms: Amy L. Best, *Prom Night: Youth, Schools, and Popular Culture* (New York, 2000); Evelyn Fairbanks, *The Days of Rondo* (St. Paul, 1990); William Graebner, *Coming of Age in Buffalo: Youth and Authority in the Postwar Era* (Philadelphia, 1990); Jane Elizabeth Hegland, "The High School Prom: A Case Study of Expectations and Dress for an American Ritual" (unpublished doctoral dissertation, University of Minnesota, 1995); and Elissa Stein and Daniel Mailliard, *Tales from the Prom* (New York, 1998).

Prom fiction is an important medium through which prom lore is passed from one generation to another: Patricia Aks, *Junior Prom* (New York, 1982); Eve Bunting, *Two Different Girls* (Mankato, Minn., 1992); Margaret Burman, *Dream Prom* (New York, 1983); Jeffrey Eugenides, *The Virgin Suicides* (New York, 1993); Diane Hoh, *Prom Date* (New York, 1996); Stephen King, *Carrie* (New York, 1974); William D. McCants, *Much Ado about Prom Night* (New York, 1995); Alix Kates Shulman, *Memoirs of an Ex-Prom Queen* (New York, 1972); Debra Spector, *Night of the Prom* (New York, 1982); Nancy Springer, ed., *Prom Night* (New York, 1999); R. L. Stine, *The Prom Queen* (New York, 1992); Todd Strasser, *Girl Gives Birth to Own Prom Date* (New York, 1996); Bobby J. G. Weiss and David Cody Weiss, *Prom Time* (New York, 1999); and Kate Williams, *Francine Pascal's Sweetwater High; a Picture-Perfect Prom?* (New York, 1998).

Index